"Good humored, intimate, and informative. . . . A contribution to knowledge."
—BROOKS ATKINSON

"A gentle, homey tale. . . . Occasionally poignant . . . never sentimental. . . . mostly sweet and sober, modest, wholesome. Here is one Peep-show that does some honor to the human race. How many new books do that?"
—NEIL MILLAR,
*Christian Science Monitor*

"Rewarding reading for anyone who has enjoyed the now classic volumes *CRY WOLF* and *RING OF BRIGHT WATER*."
—*Arizona Republic*

"Anyone who loves animals will thoroughly enjoy this."
—HELEN HOOVER, nature writer

# A Quail
# in the
# Family

WILLIAM J. PLUMMER

A FAWCETT CREST BOOK

Fawcett Publications, Inc., Greenwich, Connecticut

A QUAIL IN THE FAMILY

THIS BOOK CONTAINS THE COMPLETE TEXT OF THE
ORIGINAL HARDCOVER EDITION.

A Fawcett Crest Book reprinted by arrangement with
Henry Regnery Company

Library of Congress Catalog Card Number: 73-18176

Text illustrations by Brian Miller

Printed in the United States of America

First printing: October 1975

1   2   3   4   5   6   7   8   9   10

To all the gracious ladies
who contributed so much
in bringing Peep-Sight to print

# Contents

I like the little duck;
He doesn't know much
But he has religion. *

* *The Little Duck*
Donald Babcock
*New Yorker,* 1947

## INTRODUCTION

In writing about Peep-Sight I was spared the anguish of
the fiction writer who must carefully choose every turn of
his story from the infinite variety of his imagination. For
me, the details were already there. I had only to recall
how things had happened or to document them as they
occurred. Numerous photographs and movies assisted my
memory, and sometimes I could even observe the subject
himself. Furthermore, if I was tempted to resort to poetic
license now and then, five other memories were ready to
set me straight!

The result is this tale of a little desert quail who adopted the six of us as his family and who enriched our lives in a very special way. It needs no embellishment—it was a marvelous time, just as it happened.

And this, my friends, *is* exactly the way it happened . . .

# 1

## BEAU PEEP

It was a Saturday morning in May of 1969 and already warm, even for Las Vegas. The spring winds and blowing sand had subsided, leaving the air clean and light. In the distance, calico mountains were outlined sharply against the clear, unbroken blue, while a few blocks away the Sahara tower sparkled in the sunlight. Its flashing sign marked the start of the Strip, and against the bright sky it was barely readable as it alternately announced: *11:00—95°*. A little farther on, the Riviera and the Stardust clamored for attention; then came the new Frontier, boasting of Jimmy Durante in its show room. Frank Sinatra was appearing at Caesars Palace, and, in a penthouse atop the Desert Inn, the enigmatic Mr. Hughes was pondering additional acquisitions for his Nevada empire.

Working on the shrubs around the pool, I had stripped off my shirt to savor the southwestern sun on my midwestern back. Pausing to study the palms, their new fronds just emerging in tight accordion pleats, I shuddered a little. It was time to remove last year's growth, hanging dead and dry against the trunks, but I knew that my gloves would be useless against those hooked, shark's-tooth thorns. Still, the old fronds had to come off.

As I debated with myself, Mike, the youngest of our three boys, came slamming out into the backyard.

"Hey, Dad, I found another baby bird!"

I responded to his obvious enthusiasm with a small sigh of resignation. "Couldn't you put it back in its nest?"

"There was no nest around. He was all by himself on the ground."

As Mike came up to me and carefully uncupped his dusty hands, I expected to see the usual quasi embryo, naked and pink and wrinkled. Instead, his unfolding fingers revealed a captivating little chick the size of my thumb. He was no more than a striped fuzz-ball in beige and brown, but cute as a cartoon character. A tiny topknot was already evident, and his feet were like outsized snowshoes, almost as big as his body.

More by intuition than by recognition I exclaimed, "Why, that's not a bird, it's a quail!" The illogical distinction seemed somehow appropriate.

Mike, who was nearly nine, was genuinely surprised at my observation, but I scolded him anyway for removing wildlife from its natural environment. The fact was he had found the baby in the desert only a block away and had looked about carefully for a family before retrieving it. Apparently the chick had hatched late or had become separated through some crisis or other. It could hardly have been more than a few hours out of its shell, and easy prey for a hawk or fox.

The sudden sun dazzled the wee fellow, and he closed his eyes a moment to bask in its warmth. Then in a wink he was up and squirming to be free. Incredibly small and fragile, he was so active that we were afraid he would injure himself.

"Well, I suppose he hasn't much chance of survival," I commented, "but at this point, his only hope is with us. We'd better do our best for him."

So my gardening was put aside while Mike and I mobilized the family to accommodate our newest boarder.

In those days our house often served as an animal refuge. On any given day there was sure to be more than one small creature enjoying our care and custody. The list might include a stunned songbird deceived by an exceptionally clean picture window or a venturesome lizard rescued from the bottom of the pool. Guarding our entrance light was a great praying mantis, fattening up on miller moths, and in the den a kangaroo rat named Squeaky had resided comfortably in his special bookshelf for five years.

Although many of our little guests were wild, it was not because we lived in a remote area. Ours was a typical suburban plot in a well-established residential neighborhood, but in Las Vegas the desert is always close at hand. Like many cities in the Southwest, Las Vegas had grown by sprawling out in an irregular checkerboard pattern, leaving numerous patches of undeveloped real estate interspersed among the developments. These remained rough and rugged, lying idle while their capital value appreciated. Typically, they were sandhills covered with sage and thistle, tumbleweed, mesquite, and creosote bush, and within their boundaries wildlife flourished. No wonder that an occasional roadrunner, rabbit, or even a desert fox might cross the wrong street and crash an afternoon pool party.

At our house he'd find himself encouraged to stay. The boys were forever adopting snakes, insects, and lizards. My wife, Wanda, drew the line at scorpions and tarantulas, but even so we entered the boys' rooms with some trepidation. And anyone poking around the house late at night had better have a flashlight and slippers!

Mike's sister Leslie was our eldest, just fourteen and with appreciable experience at managing the animal ménage. Her credits included fish, frogs and turtles, hamsters and mice, parakeets, canaries, a duck, and even, briefly, a baby alligator.

It was Leslie to whom we turned now for help with Mike's foundling. She promptly produced a surplus five-

gallon aquarium. In it we deposited sand, gravel, weeds, and the baby quail, in that order. The little chick began at once to pace rapidly along the front of the glass, looking for an exit. His incessant peeping led us to christen him, rather unimaginatively, "Peep." Subsequent elaboration made it "Beau Peep," but this proved too cumbersome for regular use.

Peep understood at once how to drink water from a bottle cap, but we were temporarily at a loss to provide him with acceptable food. After a series of rejections we gained his endorsement for cherry pie filling, and eventually cornmeal and flour found his approval too. In a pinch, he seemed able to locate minuscule edibles among the litter.

By now we were a committee of six attending to the baby bird's welfare, but our combined credentials were singularly unimpressive. Despite many exposures to wildlife, we were almost completely ignorant of the ways of desert quail. We had sighted them frequently in the desert, but our observations were inevitably brief and distant. I am afraid, too, that as naturalists our approach was haphazard—rather more empirical than academic. Unless circumstances focused our interest upon a given species, we were not likely to refer to the literature.

Thus it was that none of us had any concrete idea of how to get Peep through that first night. Presumably some pseudo-maternal source of warmth was required, but we worried that he might burn or smother. We settled finally upon a cigar box wired with two small Christmas tree lights. This was propped up at one end of the enclosure with a discarded sock tacked over its open side.

As evening approached, we covered the aquarium with a towel, leaving the corners open for air and observation.

The Christmas tree bulbs provided a faint rosy glow, while steady, radiant warmth filtered through the old brown-checked sock. Peep took to the arrangement right away, sprawling up onto the box rather than nestling against it.

For the first hour or two we checked on him frequently. He appeared to be doing just fine, comfortable and content, with no evident problems. Warning ourselves that he'd probably not make it through the night anyway, we tiptoed off to watch television.

\* \* \*

Our skepticism was very likely justified. In the wild, a great many baby quail are weeded out naturally soon after hatching, and even in captivity many die in the first few days. One local breeder stated that with Gambel's quail (which we subsequently found Peep to be) only about 15 percent of any that hatch are likely to reach adolescence. Even this requires starting them out in carefully controlled brooders—disinfected with ultraviolet light, temperature maintained at 98°—and feeding them a special mash containing antibiotics. Apparently the breeders haven't discovered the power of cherry pie filling!

Beau Peep had, however, and when we uncovered his aquarium the next day, he was already up and tromping happily about in it. He looked very chipper—bright-eyed and hungry. Resuming an inventory of the pantry, we added pancake mix to his list of edibles, and he devoted the morning to eating, pacing, and napping.

We resisted the impulse to handle him, but by midafternoon we were sufficiently encouraged at his obvious vigor to take him outside. Making a little procession to the shady patio area, we arranged ourselves as an enclosure with Peep in the middle. He was delighted with his new freedom and darted about this way and that, pecking at bits of dirt and grass with great enthusiasm.

He was such a little charmer, unbelievably tiny in the huge outdoors. Tripping himself repeatedly, he raced eagerly about on his great snowshoe feet, looking for all the world like Tweetie Bird of the Warner Brothers cartoons. Peeping and pecking constantly, he managed to find minute insects on the paving, so small that we had to look closely even to see them.

It was Sunday afternoon, and our good friends Ted and Marie dropped by for their weekly visit. They were enthralled by our new foster child. Ted and I took movies to document the little bird's frenetic activities, but he moved so rapidly we could hardly keep him in view, much less in focus.

After a half hour we put him back in the aquarium, where he drank from the bottle cap and almost immediately went to sleep, atop the lighted box. By the time our friends left, he was up and pacing again, so we took him out once more in the cool twilight.

After that he was exercised several times a day, making no effort to run off. If he found himself more than a few yards from us, he came scurrying back; if we moved away, he would follow close behind until we settled into a new location. We discovered he would stay with any one of us, so we could spell each other off at quail-sitting, passing the duty from one to the other without unsettling him. Within a few days, he had explored most of the backyard, and we had seen it from an entirely new point of view. It was much larger and more interesting than we had thought.

Imperceptibly he grew. His peeping became louder and the cereals he ate became coarser; the insects he found now were easier for us to see. When the movie film returned from processing, we could scarcely believe he had been so small only a week before. Incredibly, his feet had grown too, maintaining their outlandish proportions!

He was becoming so active that we hated putting him back into the aquarium, and so we began to consider alternatives. We were reluctant to undertake anything very elaborate, being at least halfway convinced that at any moment he would be gone, one way or another. Perhaps some urge would send him off to the desert looking for his real family. More likely he would just fall ill and die, or smother in his sleep on the cigar box—by way of precaution we unscrewed one light bulb. Worse still, he might be picked off by one of the semiwild cats that were always prowling about. Of course we maintained a careful vigil over him outside, but the cats were quick and clever; Leslie had recently lost a dear guinea pig to one, in broad daylight and practically at her feet.

I was not anxious to build a permanent cage for him, nor to leave him outdoors overnight, but I could see that the five-gallon aquarium was rapidly becoming too small. Every day he became more active. Little feathers were now appearing on his stubby wings, and when he hurried to catch up to us, he assayed short, fluttering hops. We considered returning him to the desert, but he was obviously too helpless yet to make it alone. Maybe later, when he was fully grown.

A further complication arose: we had planned three separate vacation trips for the summer, and the first, to New Mexico, was scheduled to begin in about a week. Still not accepting his permanence, we decided to concern ourselves about these absences one at a time. For now, we would not plan beyond the first one. If he was still with us when that was done, well, then we'd worry about the next, and so on.

For the moment the problem was to find a larger enclosure. Chris, our oldest boy, and Leslie engaged in a complicated series of swaps that left Peep with a ten-gallon aquarium. This was some improvement: it provided him twice the room to move around. Next, we prevailed upon our neighbors to come in daily, to replenish the bottle cap and the cherry pie filling. Then finally, the night before we left, I unscrewed the remaining Christmas bulb on a trial basis. Peep appeared not to miss it, so I unplugged the cigar box altogether, thereby eliminating one more hazard.

\* \* \*

When we returned in a week, we found little Beau Peep in excellent health and voice. The neighbors had fed and exercised him regularly, and he was thriving. During our absence he had feathered out noticeably. Now he was eating grass shoots and tiny worm-like insects, as well as bread crumbs. And when we held him up a little way above the grass, he stepped off confidently and fluttered to the ground—always landing feet first, of course, for they were the heaviest part of his body

One day he discovered the pleasure of the dust bath. The newly erupting pin feathers must have itched, because the first time he found a dry, barren spot in the lawn, he began rubbing himself into it. Soon he was pecking and scratching with great abandon, fluttering his little wings and stirring up a cloud of dirt. He turned and rolled and generally enjoyed himself. It became a regular part of every outing, and gradually he developed a number of favorite spots.

By now he was spending most of his wakeful day outside the aquarium, but even returning to it to sleep was becoming impossibly confining. Our second trip was coming up, and this time Beau Peep would be without any of us for about two weeks. Preparing to depart, we were faced once more with the question of a suitable enclosure and with arrangements for his care.

Unfortunately, our neighbors were planning to be gone too, and in any case it was clear that such an active bird couldn't be restricted to a ten-gallon glass cage for any extended period. As we became concerned, Ted and Marie volunteered to put him up at their place across town. They had dogs and cats, but their enclosed back porch had good potential. Even so, we were hesitant to agree—Peep would get plenty of care and attention with our friends, but he would be an imposition on them. We were reluctant to burden them with him.

But we did.

\* \* \*

While we were vacationing in Minnesota, we came upon a delightful little book called *That Quail, Robert.*[1] It recounted the life of a bobwhite that was raised from hatch-out by a retired couple in Orleans, Massachusetts. Robert had had the run of their home like a dog or cat and became very attached and domestic. We all read it with great interest, particularly the early chapters since they had the most relevance for us. The bobwhite quail is adapted to a totally different environment from the desert, of course, but still we felt that we had found some useful reference material. Robert, however, turned out to be a female, and somehow we were all quite certain from the very beginning that Beau Peep was a male.

When we returned home this time, the change in Peep's appearance was truly remarkable. Ted and Marie had given him the very best of care, even buying him meal worms, and he had responded with good health and growth. He was now completely feathered out, still in a mottled beige and brown.

Curiously, his feathers were all too long. He looked to be wearing an overcoat several sizes too large, like a college cat from the flapper era, all decked out in a coonskin

---

[1]Margaret A. Stanger (Philadelphia: Lippincott, 1966).

coat! Then too, his head and neck were a bit scrawny looking; and despite the fact that he was finally catching up to his fabulous feet, he still had an awkward way of walking. We concluded that Beau Peep had become an adolescent bird; and sure enough, his peeping was punctuated now with occasional broken squawks.

The next time we took him to our backyard for exercise he promptly flew up to the roof. He was as surprised as we, and for a few minutes he stood tentatively at the edge, peering down at us, making querulous comments and ignoring our coaxing to return. Finally I retrieved him, and for the next few weeks this too became a regular part of our outings.

It got worse. One day he took off from the roof and flew across the street, almost into the claws of an incredulous cat, to be saved at the last moment by an alert and sympathetic neighbor. Other times he flew to the top of a cottonwood, surveying the neighborhood and practicing the mature calls that he was beginning to develop. We would watch him for a bit, and then coax him down to the roof where I could reach him from the ladder.

Each new venture increased our feeling that eventually Peep would fly off to the deert for good. We told ourselves it would be for the best, and when the time came, we should neither regret nor prevent it. But we were not anxious to hurry the day.

# 2

## VAGABOND PRINCE

It may be that the combination of ignorance and good intentions has been discredited more than it deserves. This particular combination had served Peep remarkably well thus far, and under it he had developed into an active adolescent bird.

It was now impossible to confine him even in the house. Fortunately, our high, open ceilings permitted him to get well above his surroundings—he could perch on the curtain rods, window casings, and even the center beams. After a week or so of trying various roosts, he began sleeping regularly on top of the kitchen cupboards. I installed seed and water dispensers there so that he could fly up whenever he felt the need for rest or refreshment. When it became dark outside and the kitchen lights went out, Peep put himself to bed. The cupboard tops became his home base, and the aquariums were abandoned for good.

He liked the wild bird seed that we bought; however, when outside, he supplemented his diet with insects and little green shoots. Flies were his special delicacy, but they were too fast for him to catch—one of us had to swat them for him. He thought this a marvelous game, showing great interest at the appearance of the swatter and disappointment whenever we missed.

By the time of our third and final trip of the summer, it was evident that Peep was reaching maturity. His plumage was fitting him somewhat better now; he resembled a miniature turkey. He was even beginning to achieve occasional rooster-like crowings. A dark smear of color across his eyes gave him an incongruous, sinister appearance.

From a book that described various species of desert quail we concluded that Peep was of the variety called Gambel's. The color pictures were very striking, and we were amazed and delighted at the prospect of his becoming so handsome. We looked forward to his metamorphosis.

Our last trip of the summer was to the mountains of Colorado, where our family would have a large, comfortable cabin in the midst of a pine forest. After carefully weighing the alternatives, we decided to take Peep along; we would risk his deciding to strike out on his own while we were there.

As it happened, all turned out well. Peep took to the roof a few times, but generally he stayed with us, sunning on the porch, scrounging on the grounds, or napping in the cabin. He even learned to catch an occasional fly by himself! It was a splendid outing for all of us, and Peep seemed reasonably content traveling in a cage in the car.

Returning from this last trip, we began to relax at home. The long, hot summer came to an end, and Peep set about establishing himself as a regular member of the household. Somehow it was tacitly assumed that he would live in the house with us like the bobwhite quail, Robert.

We did give one last thought to providing him a cage outside, at least as an alternative to the kitchen cupboards. After all, we said, one just doesn't keep a chicken in the house! A ready-made possibility existed in what we called the meany-olium—a sizable stationary enclosure that Chris and I had built in the backyard for lizards.

The occupants of the meany-olium seemed to find it quite comfortable. In the heat of the day, it was well shaded; at other times, there was filtered sunlight and a choice of exposure. The lawn sprinklers provided occasional dampening, and the natural sand was suitable for the nocturnal burying that some species require.

Whiptails constructed burrows under the rocks, cohabiting in apparent harmony with desert iguanas and zebra-tails. The cage was named, however, after the desert spiny lizards, which we had dubbed "meanies." These crocodile-like creatures grew to considerable size, looked very ferocious, and were in fact quite ill tempered. Equipped with dozens of sharp little teeth, a large meany could (and would) lacerate a carelessly tendered finger.

Most lizards prefer to catch their food live; however, some could be coaxed into taking morsels of raw hamburger dangled on a thread. When our reptile hostelry was filled, the boys would spend several hours each day hauling in grasshoppers, cicadas, moths, grubs, and—until Wanda found out about it—roaches.

The meanies were also prevalent in their natural state along our concrete block walls. Sometimes we witnessed boundary disputes as they came face-to-face. They puffed up and performed pigeon-toed push-ups at each other

until one or the other turned away in apparent conces-
sion. As we watched their silent confrontations, we were
reminded of familiar scenes from the Godzilla movies.

Of course, if Peep were to take over the meany-olium, it
meant evicting its present occupants and refurbishing the
interior. Somehow it didn't seem right. When we tried
him in it briefly, he was indignant at being confined while
out-of-doors. We put the idea aside, and he continued to
eat and sleep regularly atop the kitchen cupboards.

\*  \*  \*

Peep ranged freely about the house, completely at his
ease. He was endlessly curious; much of his day was spent
up on the beams and traverse rods watching our activities.
If he were sufficiently interested, he would flutter down to

join us. As he explored his fascinating world, obviously enchanted with each new discovery, we found ourselves sharing in his pleasure. Almost daily he originated some new antic to charm and to amuse us—and occasionally to our dismay.

Rob and Mike, the younger boys, began to find that he could be a nuisance. Often they were unaware of his presence until he suddenly plopped into whatever game they were playing on the floor. Then they'd push him aside or run him off. He was persistent, however; and when a clamor built up, he'd be banished to another part of the house.

Peep was't always welcome in the kitchen, either, since he loved to get into the middle of Wanda's cooking activities to look for treats. He especially liked to scratch in the flour or steal a bit of berry pie. Frequently, her crusts were vented with authentic quail tracks.

Peep never showed any interest in intruding upon us at dinner, but he liked to join us in snacks around the pool or patio. He would flutter up to the table and help himself to whatever was accessible, sometimes perching on a shoulder to ask for samples of a sandwich.

We made quite the pastoral picture as we sat outside in the early evening tending our flock. There would be Beverly, the desert tortoise—ageless, impassive, inscrutable —ruminating like a bovine. Then came Rusty, the tricolor Angora guinea pig, nibbling and darting along, zigzagging frenetically from tuft to tuft. Finally, there was Peep, taking tentative pecks at anything that came into view. Frequently he was tempted to try a strand or two of Rusty's long, colorful fur. Then Rusty's normally jerky movements became even more spasmodic until, in an effort to protect his rear, he would flip completely around to face the pesky Peep. Then Peep would just turn away and stroll nonchalantly off to see what Beverly was doing.

*     *     *

Autumn in Las Vegas is an especially enjoyable time. Often there are three or four months of perfect weather— clear, golden days with little need of heating or cooling. Except during an occasional wind, doors and windows can stand open all day. As the days grow shorter and the nights cooler, the blue sky deepens and the pyracantha berries turn bright scarlet against rich, waxy green foliage. The gray green olive trees are dotted with black fruit; clumps of pampas grass suddenly proffer exquisitely delicate plumes. Although deciduous trees turn yellow, palms and lawns remain green until the hard freezes finally hit, usually between Thanksgiving and Christmas. All in all, it is a beautiful, colorful time.

As autumn came this year, Peep's plumage deepened and sharpened, and his contours filled out. The random, mottled coloration gave way to definite markings in striking contrasts. His new feathers suited him perfectly, and his carriage began to reflect a certain pride and poise. Our ugly duckling transformed: suddenly he was a handsome, mature Gambel's rooster just like the pictures we had seen in the book.

Now we felt sure that his departure was imminent. We had attempted as conscientiously as possible to avoid becoming overly attached to him. Ultimately, we felt, he belonged to the wild—too much possessiveness now could impair his becoming self-sufficient later. Furthermore, our fondness for him might preclude our acting in his best interest. However, despite all these good intentions he had, of course, completely captivated us, and we dreaded the prospect of losing him.

Then, one evening at dusk, a flock of about thirty quail appeared in the trees in our front yard. We could scarcely believe it. It was very rare for them to enter a completely populated neighborhood; we had noted no previous instance. Perhaps they were responding to Peep's earlier calls; perhaps this was his flock and they had come for him. For a moment, I felt caught up in some bizarre version of a Friml operetta; here was the roving band of gypsies come to reclaim their vagabond prince who had been left for safekeeping as an infant at the burgomaster's doorstep!

Shaking my head a little to clear the fantasy, I brought him outside, not to release him, but to observe his reaction and theirs.

Nothing. As far as I could tell, they were completely and mutually indifferent. There appeared to be no communication; neither the quail in the trees nor Peep took any particular notice of the other. The flock soon flew back toward the desert, and Peep and I returned to the house.

We felt considerably relieved. While Peep's parents could well have been a part of that particular covey, there was no identification with them whatever. Apparently it was only chance that had brought them to our yard. Nonetheless, we found the incident somehow reassuring. A symbolic milestone had been passed. We took it to mean that Peep might remain with us for a time after all. Perhaps he would stay until spring came, and the mating season of the Gambel's quail.

# 3

## PEEP, THE SIGHT

It took some time to assimilate fully Peep's dramatic metamorphosis into maturity. Although still very active, he now was anything but awkward. His movements were more purposeful, even touched sometimes with a sort of regal grace. Perched on the traverse rod and observing activities outside, he was above it all and aloof. His occasional full-throated calls were clear and authoritative. The ragged adolescent bird had become a poised, self-confident adult.

The striking beauty of a mature Gambel's quail cannot be properly appreciated from color pictures or stuffed birds, nor for that matter, from occasional glimpses in the wild. Even a game farm does not compare with having a healthy specimen to examine at leisure. Peep at home was relaxed and natural; it was a delight to observe his bright, clean plumage at close range under good light.

The basic hue of the Gambel's quail is a glossy slate

gray with a light beige underside and a transverse stroke of black in front of the legs. The beak, eyes, and toenails are shiny black, and a combination bib and mask is black edged in white. A fine white line connects the corner of the mouth to the corner of the eye. A jet black plume, narrow at the base but full at the tip, arcs forward from the top of the head. The male's topknot plumes are generally longer, often dangling over in front of his eyes.

Males are otherwise distinguishable by a reddish-brown cap, and both sexes have russet on the sides below the wings. Taken individually, these latter feathers are especially delicate and beautiful. Each has a contrasting stroke of creamy white at its central stem, so that collectively they form a smear of rich russet flecked with ivory. The body feathers are double, each quill producing an outer, contour-feather with an insulating down-feather underneath.

Peep moulted more or less continuously—discarded feathers were often in evidence—but his plumage was always in good condition. Every month or so he produced a new topknot, which consisted of several feathers merging into a single plume. Replacements grew alternately from two separate locations about an eighth of an inch apart. They came in quickly so that he was never without a plume.

A quail's plumage is so mobile that he is quite able to deceive an observer about his true size. I was amazed to discover how small Peep's body really was. Fully grown, he had no more bulk than a robin, but he could modify his shape and size tremendously by the position of his feathers. In a normal situation, he presented the characteristic hunched shoulders and pigeon-breast, giving him a moderately heavy look. Shaking out from his dust bath or puffing up to impress, he appeared to increase his volume by half. On the other hand, at a sudden shadow in the sky, he might crouch down and flatten his feathers, becoming as small and thin as a Bohemian waxwing.

Peep actually appeared to have complete control of his feathers. I often observed him slowly rippling them out from tail to head or in the reverse order. At other times, he might just ruffle a particular patch of them to get at a loosening bit of dander.

Like most birds, Peep did not like to be held or petted. While watching television or just napping, he would sit on my leg or my ankle as comfortable as a kitten. However, if I attempted to stroke him, he stood up and hopped off. I sometimes confined him in my hands, gently rubbing his head or scratching his neck. He seemed to enjoy this and wouldn't struggle to get free, but neither would he tarry when released. Instead, he would hasten to rearrange any feathers I might have rumpled or to remove imagined specks of dirt.

Peep was very systematic and meticulous about preening. He spent several hours every day applying the natural oil from the gland at the base of his tail to the full length of each feather. This exercise was facilitated by a neck that could be almost serpentine, enabling him to reach nearly anywhere on his body with his beak. His contortions were amusing to watch. Without changing position he could inspect himself from any direction—even behind or below!

Having become an adult, Peep knew he was handsome and became fastidious about his appearance. He disliked having any extraneous material on him. If he stepped into Leslie's oil paints, or stuck something to the bottom of a foot, he became obsessed and would work at the foreign substance until every trace had been removed.

He was so neat and clean that visitors often asked if he was housebroken. He was not, although the question was reasonable. As a matter of fact, I'm sure Peep contributed very little household dirt. With rare exceptions, his droppings were solid and dried quickly without staining; they were easily picked up with tissue or whisked into a dustpan. The cupboard tops were cleaned daily whenever fresh seeds and water were provided. Peep had his favorite haunts—on the window sills, on the kitchen chairs, or under the table—and we all fell into the habit of cleaning up after him; thus, it was never a major chore for anyone. Of course, when he had spent an afternoon on my desk or dresser, there was no mistaking the fact.

Despite his innate cleanliness, we never entirely lost our self-consciousness at having a "chicken" living free in the house. Still, we found no reason to believe that he carried disease or had any vermin on his body. His health was excellent and his appearance well groomed.

Peep became so dedicated to maintaining his impeccability that it was a surprise when he abandoned it, even temporarily. One day Wanda was working about the kitchen on some cakes or pies, and in the midst of her machinations, she was called to the phone. Returning, she found that Peep had walked through the batter and was now enjoying a dust bath in the flour! Her laughter and cries of dismay brought the family running, and Peep was surprised to find himself suddenly the complete center of attention. As he drew himself up and shook self-consciously, he lost his balance and slipped into the flour, thereby completing the debacle.

Wanda exclaimed, "Well, Peep, you are really a sight!"

Mike concurred, "That's him all right, Peep, the sight."

We all agreed, and soon we were calling him Peep-Sight.

We wiped and brushed off the worst of his mess and then let him retire to the cupboard tops to finish the job privately. Within a few hours he had removed every trace of flour and dishabille, but somehow his new name stuck to him for good. Little Beau Peep had become Peep-Sight, and so he remained from that day on.

*     *     *

Despite our having had many previous pets, the relationship that Peep was developing with us was very special and quite unexpected. It was entirely unlike any we had ever enjoyed with other wild creatures, and yet it certainly was not that of the usual domestic animal, either.

No matter how close a dog is to his master, he always accepts his role as a valued but inferior friend or servant. A cat is likely to maintain great independence and aloofness, often viewing himself as the master to be served. Neither description approximated Peep-Sight's relationship with us.

Sometimes, upon adopting a wild pet, one may bring along a bit of the animal's habitat to make him feel more comfortable—a little natural island set in the ordered domestic environment. We had done this in making a place for Squeaky, the kangaroo rat, in his Lion Country bookshelf. It was complete with rocks and tunnels, food and water, and subdued lighting for his nocturnal activities. Since kangaroo rats are almost totally antisocial, this exclusive and isolated arangement suited Squeaky just fine.

Although his built-in bookshelf was partially screened to discourage egress, he could easily escape if he wished; and every now and then, he turned up unexpectedly in the middle of the night, hopping and scurrying about on some foray or other. In the morning, we recaptured him as he slept in the couch springs or a corner of the closet and returned him unresisting to his proper home. We suspected that he sometimes completed these excursions without detection, although getting back up to his shelf must have been difficult for him.

Toward the end Squeaky slowed down considerably. Then, one day we discovered him lying lifeless in his favorite sleeping jar, among the walnut shells and shredded rocks that he was always transferring from one location to another. He had apparently expired quietly in his sleep.

He had lived with us as an adult for over five years, a remarkable longevity for this fascinating little desert rodent.

But Peep's circumstances were in no way similar to Squeaky's. There was no part of the house that we had modeled after his desert; nor was he in any sense isolated. He was neither caged nor wild.

The truth is that Peep-Sight was not really a pet in the usual sense at all—he was an adopted member of the household. Our home was his home, and we were his family. I'm sure *he* understood it this way from the beginning; it took the rest of us a little longer.

\*     \*     \*

Growing up in Wisconsin in the late thirties, I had enjoyed hunting a variety of game. Ecological arguments were not yet popular, and shooting was then a generally approved form of recreation. Although bobwhite quail were native to the area, the severe climate limited their numbers. They were infrequently seen, and there was no season on them—we hunted ducks, pheasants, and partridge. In the Southwest, mourning doves provide excellent shooting in early fall; and after moving to this area I had become quite enthusiastic about hunting them. Doves are plentiful and very challenging targets, and despite their small size, they are good eating.

My usual hunting partner was Rick, the son of our good friends Ted and Marie, who was likely, at any one time, to be keeping a sidewinder or desert rattler at home for observation. He often provided our boys with harmless snakes of the less common varieties. A tireless sportsman and naturalist, Rick enjoyed going home by way of the desert to check his live traps when he got off the late shift at the Flamingo Hotel, and it was he who had brought us Squeaky.

Rick and I did most of our dove hunting on a managed preserve at Overton, north of Las Vegas. Once or twice, when the dove season was over, we had hunted quail there with modest success. Naturally, as this season approached, I wondered whether having Peep-Sight in the family was going to make dove shooting an emotional conflict for me.

I suppose I might have found reasons not to go, but I had long since promised Chris, who was almost thirteen, that he could start hunting with us that fall. He had bought a gun and was not going to be put off.

As it turned out, we had a good season and Chris proved to be an excellent shot. We had no difficulty separating our relationship with Peep-Sight from the shooting of doves. Doves are quite unlovable and even vicious in terms of their social activities. As we dressed them out on the patio, Peep-Sight watched and commented, keeping enough distance to avoid possible vermin. We began bringing back special weed seeds for him from the game preserve.

In a few weeks the dove hunting was over, but Rick was not yet through putting us to the test. About the middle of October, he called to propose a quail hunt. Chris and I hemmed and hawed a bit but finally agreed. This time we were truly apprehensive about our feelings. We went, but we were not surprised at how it turned out—we had become too attached to Peep to be that indifferent to his kind. We called it a season.

In later years when we returned to Overton for dove shooting, the boys and I found we could hear the quail around us, sometimes close, sometimes at a great distance. By then we knew and recognized many of their calls, and it was as though we were eavesdropping on their private conversations. We could visualize them: how they looked, what they were saying and doing. Before Peep-Sight, their furtive comments would have gone unnoticed, but now the stealthy sounds stood out clearly, as familiar and understandable to us as the distant dialogue of other hunters. Occasionally one of us offered an answering comment. No one else noticed, but the quail sometimes responded with low-pitched replies. Then we would exchange sly secret looks, taking great satisfaction in our privileged communication.

*    *    *

At Christmas time, Peep-Sight was enchanted by all the special activity, the decorations, and especially the Christmas tree. Our sunken living room and open-beam ceilings permitted a tall tree, and he flew up into it to help with the trimming. He enjoyed perching in the branches, nibbling at the tinsel, and posing like the partridge in the pear-tree greeting cards. On Christmas morning he bustled about in the wrappings, investigating and admiring each new toy. His lively interest made it special for all of us.

That winter my job required considerable travel, flying to Boston or Washington every week or two for several days' business. I found myself regaling my associates with tales of Peep and his exploits. Smehow the thought of a desert quail living free in a sunny house in Nevada relieved the oppressive chill and gloom of the dreary eastern winter. I was cheered at the thought of returning to hear of his latest escapades, just as one might anticipate the antics of a new grandson. Arriving at the airport, I felt a moment's apprehension and prepared for the possibility that he had met with some accident during my absence, or that he had finally decided to strike out on his own. But reaching home, I was invariably relieved to find him in good health and spirits, greeting me casually as though I had been gone only a few hours.

With February came the crocuses and the anemones and then the spring winds. We watched Peep-Sight for evidence of wanderlust, but none appeared. He continued just as he was, settled and at home with his family, ingenuous and unconcerned.

Spring is brief in southern Nevada, and before we knew it, it was summer again. Las Vegas summers are long and sizzling. Often the temperature reaches 100° by mid-morning, and daily highs of 110° for extended periods are not uncommon. However, it is not humid, and, as long as there is air movement, one can be surprisingly comfortable outside by simply avoiding heavy exertion and direct sunlight. Native wildlife recognizes this instinctively and, for much of the day, is prudently quiescent, dozing in the shade or buried in cool sand.

Peep-Sight spent most of his day in the house, but he did enjoy an occasional outing, browsing in the flowerbeds or under the palms, maintaining a leisurely pace and keeping to the shade. He might rest for a moment under the chaise and then, spotting a root beer or a Coke, would ask for a drink. If he was in the sun too long, he would open his beak and pant like a dog. We took this as a warning to get him back into the air-conditioned house.

For some time, Peep-Sight was oddly attracted by the pool. When we were in it, he seemed to envy our pleasure at swimming and to contemplate joining us. When one of us talked to him from the water, he came to the edge and appeared on the verge of hopping in. Then, afraid of the consequences, we'd distract him by letting him drink from a cupped hand or pouring water at his feet. We had a narrow escape one afternoon when something alarmed him. He flew across the pool, almost touching down on it but then continued on to the other side. Since a quail is not aerodynamically agile, we were afraid that even one feather-wetting splash would have quickly made a sinker of him.

Despite our concern, that summer Peep-Sight enjoyed backyard boat rides. It started one day when he spotted

Chris sunning on an air mattress, drifting about in the pool. Peep came up to the edge in his interested way and began addressing Chris. Chris paddled over and invited him aboard, and Peep promptly hopped over to Chris's foot. Chris then shoved off, and the bird seemed quite satisfied to amble about on Chris's legs and abdomen, touring the pool. As he strutted about, Peep looked like a feathery Captain Bligh on the deck of the *Bounty*—casual, confident, and in complete command! When Peep finally became restive, Chris simply paddled back to the embarkation point and put his foot to the edge again; Peep

marched ashore and back to his other interests. The episode was repeated a number of times during the summer without accident.

By late summer it dawned on us that Peep-Sight had been an adult now for nearly a year, and perhaps he was going to stay after all. He was obviously at home with us, and unless he felt some urgings this autumn, he must surely be established here for good.

It was all very encouraging, but there was just one catch. We had decided to move.

# 4

## A NEW HOUSE

Our move was several miles across town into a new development. The house was a semi-Spanish, single-story stucco with a low, pitched roof and enough bedrooms for everyone. A concrete block wall enclosed the sizeable backyard but left an excellent view of the western mountains and the now distant, glittering Strip. To one side was the pool, and at the other we planned a patch of elevated lawn bordered by shrubs and flowers with a casual suggestion of formality.

It was our first new house, and we had put everything into it. Our resources had run out, however, short of the landscaping. At the old place there had been shade and mature vegetation everywhere; here we stood starkly exposed amidst sand and thistle. For the next year, Chris and I worked every free hour to put in planters, retaining walls, lawn, sprinklers, shrubs, and trees. Meanwhile, Peep-Sight gradually took over the interior.

He made the basic transfer without serious difficulty. We brought him over last—after the furniture was in place and the commotion had subsided. At first, it was just another adventure like a ride in the car or a Christmas tree in the house. When the novelty wore off, he was a little lost; but finally he began to settle down.

Peep was, however, bothered by the conventional low ceilings. He repeatedly flew up to look for perches that would provide him his accustomed elevation, but there were none. He walked the length of each traverse rod, picking his way carefully over the drapery rings, but they were jammed up too close to the ceiling. There was no space for him on the kitchen cupboards either; they extended all the way to the ceiling. Finally, to replace his cupboard tops, I installed a high shelf complete with seed and water dispensers to help him through the initial accommodation. It wasn't long until he had accepted the new situation and abandoned the shelf as unnecessary.

We established a regular feeding spot for him on the kitchen counter near the pass-through window to the patio. His feeder was a discarded puzzle box with fine sandpaper in the bottom and a jigger of fresh water alongside. The sides of the box minimized scatter to the counter, while the sandpaper lining helped to keep his beak and toenails trimmed. We added seeds every morning, and he flew up several times a day to scratch and peck in his box.

Eventually he selected as his permanent roost the top of a seven-foot highboy in the dining room, opposite the door to the kitchen. Finding a flowerpot there, he forcibly evicted the unfortunate occupant and appropriated the pot for his indoor dust baths.

It was quite a long time before he had familiarized himself with every room in the house. At the beginning he spent most of his day in the family room and the kitchen; then he started napping under a convenient table in the dining room or the living room. Finally, he began to venture occasionally into the bedrooms as well. The bathrooms came last.

Outside, Peep stayed near the patio at first but eventually ranged to the limits of the backyard. With his natural curiosity, he might have continued expanding his territory had we permitted. From time to time, he flew up to the roof or the wall—and occasionally to the neighbors' yard. We consistently discouraged this and retrieved him promptly. We declared the front yard off limits too, and in time he accepted the boundaries we set.

It took us all a while to become accustomed to the new house and the new neighborhood; we had been quite settled in our former location. Peep adapted as quickly as any of us, and in due time, we were all reestablished in our daily routines.

\*   \*   \*

Peep-Sight's daily routine included a lot of sleeping. A typical day began as early as 6:30 or 7:00 A.M., and ended about 10:00 P.M. He started with a sort of morning shower—a leisurely dust bath in the liberated flowerpot. After coming down to a moderate breakfast at the seed tray, perhaps he'd retire for his first nap in a corner of the dining room, staying out of traffic while the household cleared out. Sometimes he went to the living room window instead and watched the neighborhood kids off to the corner bus stop. At such times, his first nap was beneath the glass-top coffee table where the morning sunshine streamed in through the front windows.

Since his day was exceptionally long, I suppose it was natural for Peep to spend much of it asleep. Even with a much shorter active period, most animals nap several times during the day. Peep lived in a comfortable air-conditioned house, but he still liked his siestas.

He employed a surprising variety of sleeping positions. His favorite position for catnapping was simply to fold his legs under, facing forward with head pulled in and feathers fluffed out, forming a comfortable little pile. He preferred this posture for the arm or back of an upholstered chair, but it was especially used on the carpeted floors where he liked to "covey up" between a pair of shoes.

On a desk or dresser top, Peep would doze off standing on both feet. Eventually, he would tuck up one leg so that

it disappeared completely and balance himself on the other with the help of his tail feathers just barely touching some adjacent surface. All fluffed out with beak on bosom and topknot laid low, he became a feathery little sphere on a pedestal. Occasionally, he'd rouse himself long enough for a full-beaked yawn or a quiet little chirp.

Peep's most unusual position was to lie on his side with his limbs stretched out, like a hound dog on the hearth. He responded in this way to direct sunlight or to other radiant heat sources such as the movie light. In the hot sun, he soon roused himself from this position and moved to a cool shady spot. Once, however, while using the movie lights in filming, we were shocked to see a curl of smoke rise from his plumage! Needless to say, we became more careful thereafter.

For serious napping, Peep-Sight tucked his head under a wing. I don't believe he did this when alone or when he retired for the night, but in the daytime with the family, it signified that he was really tired.

Peep-Sight often napped while viewing television. He seemed to enjoy watching and spent a great deal of time looking at the screen. Generally, he took a position across the room on the sofa or someone's knee, facing toward the set. If Wanda or Leslie were ironing in the family room, he liked to sit at one end of the board watching the tube and dozing. Even when he was alone, Peep might sit on the cushion of an armchair and watch for hours. He showed no recognition or preference for program or content, but he clearly enjoyed having the set on. Surely it was no more than an audio-visual jumble to him (as it often is to me), but it obviously provided something. In other rooms, he appreciated the sound of the radio or record player.

Peep put himself to bed about 10:00 P.M., never before, usually stopping off first for a late dinner at the feeder. If we tried to put him up earlier, he simply flew back down. On the infrequent occasions when we all retired early, "putting the bird up" was our final action. Once the lights were out and the house was quiet, he'd stay put.

On rare occasions, Peep spent the night in his flowerpot. All that was visible was the tip of his tail at one end and his plume sticking up at the other. His customary position, however, was standing on one leg next to the pot and facing out into the room. Directly under his roosting place, a low wattage bulb in a lamp in the highboy provided night-light illumination. When I arose in the wee hours to check on the house, he acknowledged my passing with a barely audible chirp or two. Considering his great powers of recognition, we wondered what might happen if a burglar should come by. I'm sure Peep would have raised a considerable outcry, but fortunately, we had no occasion to find out.

*     *     *

Once we were settled into the new house, Peep-Sight sought to assume a share of the responsibility for its management. With his keen facility for observation and a naturally cautious outlook, he gravitated toward the field of security. Soon he was screening every activity for potential threat to the safety of the household. Spending a considerable part of every day at the various windows, he monitored activities outside and warned us when something out of the ordinary was shaping up. An unfamiliar vehicle pulling up in front of the house warranted a moderate outburst, while anyone but ourselves on the back wall would provoke a string of staccato comments.

Always an intent and interested observer, he would even remark offhandedly on the movements of birds and lizards in the yard. His perception of what belonged and what didn't, inside or out, was truly remarkable. With four active teen-agers and their friends coming and going, the place was usually in considerable turmoil. Furniture, groceries, clothing—all could come and go without comment; but at anything truly unusual, he would warn us that it needed checking out.

Peep's recognition of family and friends was excellent too, and he was never deceived for more than a moment by unusual circumstances, new apparel, wigs, or haircuts. However, if a stranger had entered without his knowledge, he hurried to investigate at the first sound of the unfamiliar voice. Bustling brusquely into the room, he would circle the newcomer a few times, commenting all the while. If the visitor were fairly relaxed and calm, Peep might walk off in a moment and ignore him—this meant the stranger had passed security inspection but was not a special guest. Sometimes Peep stayed to keep an eye on things or to join in the socializing.

Generally, Peep-Sight noted the arrival of visitors before they gained entry. Hearing the doorbell, he would march officiously to the front entrance to make his evaluation. He was the examiner in charge of credentials, and they were applicants for admission. If the door was not answered promptly, he moved to a chair by the front window and peered out for preliminary scrutiny.

We tolerated but did not encourage this role of gatekeeper. While it did have value, it could also be awkward. We were never quite sure how he would react to an adult visitor. If he was not comfortable about somebody, he could be a pest.

Sometimes Peep would obviously decide to make someone unwelcome. Then his movements quickened and he became raucous and threatening. In one mode he was deceptive—he would begin edging up gradually in a disarming way with the appearance of being interested in something else altogether, and then suddenly he would attack from close range.

When he charged, he held his wings slightly out, feathers fluffed, and head down. With his open beak revealing

an angry, red mouth, he resembled a hissing cat or snake. The effect is hard to appreciate until one can actually experience six ounces of righteously wrathful quail suddenly streaking at him with obviously violent intent! I doubt that Peep could do serious injury, but we often remarked that we were happy he didn't weigh 180 pounds.

It was hard to tell what characteristics Peep found unacceptable in people. He did appear to impose some general criteria: he was likely to accept females and to reject males; house guests were usually accepted at once; and both grandmas were taken in immediately and without question. On the other hand, the younger boys' friends were lumped into a general category of trivial annoyances and were simply scolded or chased perfunctorily through the house.

For some reason, Peep-Sight resented Ted for a long time. In particular, he liked to sneak up to attack Ted's ears as we sat at cocktails. Ted was relaxed and casual, soft-spoken, and quite fond of Peep; yet something there just wasn't right. Sometimes frankly malicious, Peep would sidle up with his wings a little out and his head high, side-stepping and chip-ing frequent warnings. Once or twice, Ted had poked a finger at him to fend him off. This seemed to constitute a counterchallenge, and Peep remembered it that way. Unfortunately, his memory did not appear to extend to the care Ted and Marie had lavished on him when he was only a few months old! After several years, this hostility gradually diminished until Ted was finally accepted as a regular. After that, only a brief ceremony was required at each visit, to be sure that Ted wasn't taking anything for granted.

When we had guests, we sometimes confined Peep in one of the boys' rooms to avoid embarrassment or annoyance. He always accepted his banishment graciously, putting his time to good use and showing no resentment whatever. Upon release, he'd make a quick check to be sure the intruder had gone; then he would forget the entire episode and resume his normal duties.

Even though Peep-Sight acted as self-appointed security officer for the household, we had to remain constantly alert on behalf of his own safety. He chased after the younger boys whenever they passed by him, and it was difficult for them to avoid kicking or stepping on him. Possibly he was provoked by their rapidly moving feet in the same way that a yard dog is provoked by the rotating tires of a passing automobile. When either of the boys walked through a room, Peep was likely to dart out suddenly at one foot and then the other. Colliding with his target, he'd pick himself right up and go undaunted for the next one as it swung by.

Peep was most strongly inclined to charge at the younger boys, whose activities he disapproved in principle anyway. If anything flopped or dangled at their ankles, they could never get by unnoticed. Only with short pants, smooth-fitting socks, and neatly tied laces, had they any chance of making it. He almost never attacked my feet or Wanda's. Leslie and Chris were also less susceptible; sometimes when he did attack, they would stop to reprimand him or to pick him up to scold him. He was never deterred for long, however, by a reprimand or by an inadvertent kick.

Outside, even with established limits to his territory, we did not feel safe in leaving Peep unattended. Special hazards included BB guns, occasional dogs, and even a roadrunner who scouted the neighborhood periodically. Another danger lived next door, a black female cat named

"Ace" (whom we optimistically called "Spayed"). Hawks were also not uncommon. One summer, a nighthawk came dipping by each evening just at sunset to scoop a drink from the pool. He'd always make several passes at the surface, giving Peep a few anxious moments; then he'd swoop away to his nocturnal adventures.

Eventually, Peep-Sight seemed to comprehend the nature of the pool and to recognize that it wasn't for him. He still came to its edge for a word or a drink while we were swimming, but he no longer showed any desire to join in. However, he did enjoy harassing the younger boys and their friends as they swam, and he found it particularly satisfying to stand at the edge and hurl insults and profanities at them. We discouraged this practice as being hazardous to his health.

*　　*　　*

Peep-Sight's marvelous powers of observation convinced us that all of his senses were highly developed. His remarkable hearing and vision did not surprise us, but we often observed reactions that could only be explained by an acute sense of smell. Without relying on taste or visual inspection, he could quickly detect and reject food that was detrimentally old, adulterated, or damp; and he could obviously smell concealed chocolate at a considerable distance. He also appeared to possess a fine discrimination in the sense of taste, often selecting only certain portions or varieties of foods.

Peep-Sight was sensitive to temperatures, but this sensitivity seemed to be limited to cold items. Although he liked ice cream and soft drinks, he rejected most other foods if they came directly from the refrigerator, even when they were otherwise very attractive to him. In this case, he would circle around the item and shake his head or sneeze, but he would not partake. If it were lettuce or some other green, I would wash it in warm water and dry it for him, and then he would devour it with great relish.

Oddly, his sensitivity to temperatures did not warn him away from extremes of heat; in fact, as we had noted earlier with the movie lights, radiant heat appeared to have a dangerously soporific fascination for him. On two occasions he flew into a frying pan of hot grease. The first time, we were caught so unaware that it took a few seconds to react and rescue him. He made no effort to extricate himself but just stood there burning the bottoms of his feet. He limped about pathetically for several days but appeared to suffer no permanent impairment.

We supposed that his keen senses greatly facilitated the identification of familiar objects and people, and may even have accounted for some of his predisposition to accept or reject visitors. Because of this ability we could never be sure whether he actually responded to his name —he may have merely sensed whatever it was that we wanted. Generally, if we had a treat for him, he came readily; but when called to pose for a picture, for example, he was unresponsive.

Although his eyesight was undoubtedly extremely good, his instincts sometimes took precedence. On the glass-top coffee table, he could not bring himself to walk on the transparent surface but had to fly across instead, a distance of some eighteen inches! He could see the supporting frame at each edge but could not trust what he saw in between.

Coupled with his excellent perception, Peep-Sight had a tremendous capacity to learn. Every new experience

modified his subsequent behavior. His retention was phe-
nomenal—one could observe his constant generalizing
from the specific and discriminating from the general. As
the behaviorists put it, he was always "in process." Often
he drew conclusions that were questionable by our standards, but one could never fault his basic capability.

# 5

## LOVE'S LABORS LOST

It was inevitable that we would consider the idea of a mate for Peep-Sight, and it eventually became a perennial topic of discussion. The more seriously we explored it, however, the more complex the problem appeared.

In the first place, there was some question of whether he would accept a mate at all, since he had been raised in complete isolation from his kind. We didn't know what had transpired before Mike found him, but we assumed that he had hatched late and alone and never saw another quail until he was grown. Would he relate to his species at all?

The popular works of Robert Ardrey, Konrad Lorenz, and Desmond Morris describe the phenomenon of "imprinting," the process by which newly hatched birds form attachments and identification with whatever approximates a mother during their first few days of life. When they mature, they seek mates that resemble their "mothers." This suggests that Peep-Sight might expect to mate with an old sock! Perhaps the idea is far-fetched, but it could account for his peculiar behavior toward clothing of a certain pattern, color, or texture—and even toward shoes and feet.

Perhaps more serious than a possible identification with inanimate objects was his lack of exposure to others of his kind. One breeder of our acquaintance hatched quail in an incubator, finding that captive adults would neither nest nor care for their young. Still, his chicks grew up around other quail and apparently mated successfully when released.

Nonetheless, we were not seriously deterred by Peep's presumed lack of appropriate imprinting. Maybe we were unjustifiably optimistic, but we felt that if other conditions were suitable, surely he and a mate would develop a satisfactory association.

It was the other conditions that were major obstacles. We felt it would be practically impossible to locate an adult female presently in circumstances comparable to Peep's. The prospect of taming one, even one raised on a game farm, appeared almost as remote. Yet if she were to be a friend of Peep's, she would have to be tame and have free run of the place just as he had. The alternative of caging them both was unthinkable.

Sometimes while we were semiseriously exploring a plan, we paused for a moment to consider what it might be like if we were to succeed. Having one quail "living in" was a bit of a burden and a responsibility; keeping a pair could be much worse. For a start, there would be twice as many droppings and feathers. We could also envision the two of them calling back and forth through the house or spooking each other into wild flight, getting into things together or ganging up on visitors, or even conducting their private domestic affairs indiscreetly.

This last led to further speculation. We were told that Gambel's quail will not breed in captivity, but would such a duo consider themselves captive? We could find ourselves with a nesting pair in the house, and then with a whole family. The idea of a line of quail weaving Indian file through the place like a string of little bowling pins was both ludicrous and appalling! At this point the discussion typically fell apart. While we agreed that finding an acceptable mate was a desirable possibility, the prospect of progeny was just too much.

\* \* \*

In considering the possibility of a mate for Peep, we found ourselves speculating about his view of himself in relation to us. It was not very helpful to say that he thought of himself as a person or of us as quail. It was true that he had never evinced any interest in our other birds; they might as well have been fixtures. But what was his concept of our family structure and of his position in it? We could only guess. In any case, it was a workable one.

His special behavior toward Mike and Rob suggested a particular relationship with them. In the natural state, we are told, the roosters in the covey quarrel and bicker incessantly, chasing and bullying each other all day long. We confirmed this by watching the "real quail" in the desert through binoculars. Peep appeared to place the younger boys in this rival-like role, and perhaps they provided an outlet for his intra-special aggressiveness. Another possibility is that he understood their subadult status and felt some responsibility for curbing their youthful exuberance; it wasn't until he was fully grown himself that he began haranguing them. In either case, he

was perfectly consistent about it; he even included their friends in his diatribes.

It is more difficult to postulate his relationship to the rest of us. Infrequently he behaved in an aggressive way toward the older children, but generally they enjoyed more acceptance. Wanda and I appeared to occupy an elder status.

He clearly preferred mature company, and when things weren't too busy he often came to our room or to Chris's or Leslie's, just to visit. He might stand around and observe what we were doing, or fly up to a window sill, remarking conversationally on what he saw outside. Sometimes he simply settled in for a catnap on the dresser, making an occasional drowsy chirp or cluck as we went about our business. At these times he seemed quite charming, almost affectionate. Of course, he wouldn't permit us to pet him, but he always seemed to appreciate a compliment—he liked being told that he was a handsome bird (it confirmed his own view).

One thing was clear: Peep viewed himself as an adult member of the flock and expected to be treated accordingly. From the time of his maturity, he placed great value on his dignity and self-esteem, and we made a point of respecting it. Teasing or ridiculing him was not tolerated, nor would we allow any demeaning treatment. I believe he could tell at once if someone were making fun of him, and he expressed his resentment. Anyone who took the risk of kidding him a little could expect a sharp reply in return!

I suppose I probably put the most effort into communicating with Peep and protecting his welfare, and his behavior toward me reflected this. He and I came to regard each other with a great deal of affection and respect.

*   *   *

One autumn day in 1971, we had an opportunity to test the taming approach. I came home to find a new addition: a female Gambel's quail with a broken wing, a broken leg, and missing most of her tail feathers. She was a mess, yet somehow her beauty was still intact. A couple of the neighborhood teen-agers, who had been "dirt-hauling" on their cycles, had come upon her in the desert and brought her to us for treatment. One couldn't help wondering how much of her condition had resulted from her rescue.

She was so completely wild and unreachable that it only dramatized our remarkable rapport with Peep-Sight. It was doubtful that anything like it could even be approached with her. Before we could think of these possibilities, however, her injuries had to be treated. Since small, wild animals are generally outside the practice of most veterinarians, we felt that our own experience would be as useful as anything.

She was assigned to Peep's former aquarium and supplied with food and water. Despite her disabilities, she began the inevitable pacing, dragging one leg and wing pitifully behind, searching for escape. We covered the aquarium with a board so she could rest.

The next day we devised a splint for her leg, using toothpicks and gauze impregnated with plaster. Wanda's training as an RN served us well. In no time our little cripple was hobbling about on her cast looking considerably better, and we were encouraged to do something for the wing.

Clipping off a few feathers, we exposed the break; only

the skin held the pieces together. We attempted a splint and then bound the wing to her body, but she quickly worked it off. Our luck the next day was no better—she wouldn't leave the splint alone. Finally, we settled for simply taping the wing against her body, hoping that the ends of bone would heal together.

As the days went by, she was active and took nourishment but remained as alien and frightened of us as ever. After three weeks, we removed the cast and returned her to the darkened aquarium. In a short time, the leg appeared fully functional.

The wing, however, had not healed well. Although there was no infection, it appeared that she would not fly again. We concluded, after a few more days, that the best thing to do was to release her. We felt that taming her was out of the question, and there was no point to keeping her any longer.

We drove to the area in which the boys had found her and discovered a flock of quail! It seemed quite likely that they were her covey, but it probably didn't matter. We resisted romantic speculation as we turned her loose, and she went scurrying and fluttering off in their general direction—it was obvious that she was still a wild bird.

We felt that we had done our best for her. Even if she weren't accepted right away, she'd probably survive easily if the winter were not too severe. It was already November; perhaps in a few months she would find a mate, raise some chicks, and rejoin the flock in late summer.

We like to think that's how it turned out.

*     *     *

We were now convinced that any mate for Peep-Sight would have to be raised in the family almost from hatching as he had been. This would be no simple undertaking. First, there was the matter of timing. As far as we knew, fertile quail eggs were available only a month or so each year. We would have only these few weeks each summer during which to initiate a plan. Second, we had the problem of identifying a female. The sex of a chick is not distinguishable until it is at least three weeks old. Thus, if the process were to begin at hatch-out, we could not know the sex of the chick we had selected until we were

already committed to raising it. We could only trust to luck to produce a mate instead of a rival! Finally, there was that low survival rate. Could cherry pie filling do it again?

We were discouraged by the complexity. Only a fortuitous set of circumstances had produced a Peep-Sight in the first place. It would take an even more fortuitous set to provide him a mate.

One simple proposal attempted to reconcile the difficulties. At the appropriate time, we would obtain several eggs or newly hatched chicks and raise them all, relying on probability to provide at least one female. After those critical first few weeks, we could select the bride-to-be and continue with her alone. That took care of both the sex identification and the need to start at hatch-out; it didn't do much for the problem of survival. Having chosen a chick, we could only do our best to get her through those vulnerable first weeks. If we failed, we'd have to wait at least a year to try again.

The plan had some merit, but unfortunately it added a new problem: the disposal of the unchosen chicks. Perhaps we could give them to friends or cage them outside—but we didn't like either of those ideas. And we would never have the heart to turn them back to the game farm or the wild. With this approach, we really *could* end up with a family! Furthermore, the breeder was not anxious to provide us fertile eggs or newly hatched chicks anyway, not having great confidence in our methods.

This plan was rejected, and the problem remained open and unresolved. While we still were discouraged, we didn't completely abandon the idea. As the winter wore on, we discussed the subject from time to time; however, no action could be taken for several months—we had till summer to think about it. Peep-Sight would be three years old then and in his prime.

# 6

## A QUAIL IN RESIDENCE

In January of 1972, I began a year's leave from my work to attend the local university full time. Wanda took a job at the hospital while I took over management of the household.

Since the graduate courses were given mostly at night, my studying was done during the daytime. In the morning, when everyone had gone off to work or school, Peep-Sight and I had the house to ourselves. We cleaned up the kitchen, did a few chores outside, and then settled into the den for several hours of homework.

Peep obviously enjoyed the quiet companionship of our days together, and so did I. I loaded the phonograph, and he joined me at my desk. As I studied, he spent his time dozing on a shelf or resting against a stack of texts like a feathery bookend. Sometimes he came over to scratch for imaginary seeds on the open pages or to peck at the tip of my pen as I wrote. Occasionally, upon leaving the room, I returned to find him sitting on the seat of my chair and facing the desk in apparent caricature of myself.

While working and thinking in pursuit of scholastic goals, I also began to contemplate writing about Peep-Sight. We had talked for some time of documenting his story. Numerous photographs would remind us of our treasured times with him, but perhaps something more was warranted. Perhaps his was a tale of general interest. It was an unusual relationship, certainly, and ought to be worth putting into words. Soon I was turning frequently from my textbooks to scribble a few notes about Peep-Sight.

Some days instead of studying, I would be off to the grocery store or to the university, leaving Peep to retire for a quiet nap by himself. Taking advantage of my need to be at the library, I began looking for books on the Gambel's quail. There were very few, but I eventually uncovered an excellent study which provided insight into many of our earlier observations.[2] It confirmed a great deal of what we had surmised, but it held a few surprises too. The writer had observed a readiness on the part of quail parents to accept orphans and of coveys to accept strangers. This meant that, given the right circumstances, Peep-Sight might not have perished after all. Had we returned him to the desert, there was a remote chance of his finding foster parents there. The study also showed that a covey normally stays persistently within its established range and roosting area, straying but a few hundred yards afield and relocating only in extreme circumstances. Had

---

[2]David M. Gorsuch "Life History of the Gambel Quail in Arizona," University of Arizona Biological Science Bulletin No. 2 (Tucson: May 15, 1934).

we known, we needn't have been so concerned about his striking out on his own. Since he liked it with his family, his natural inclination was to stay with us. There were other misapprehensions too, but on the whole, our combination of ignorance and good intentions had served us surprisingly well.

As the semester progressed, I continued to add to my random observations about Peep, dropping them into a desk drawer without review or revision. Before long I had collected a considerable amount of commentary about his general behavior, and about what it was like to have a quail in the family.

\* \* \*

A great many of my notes dealt with Peep-Sight's feeding habits, which were varied and remarkable. Insects had been prominently featured in his juvenile diet, but once fully grown, he rarely ate them. The diversity of his intake created a strong impression that he balanced his diet himself. While we worried about his eating the wrong things, he appeared to maintain himself in excellent condition. His preferences were variable but always definite. We were forced to conclude that he knew what was good for him and what was needed at any particular time.

Peep's staples were several commercial bird feed mixes that we alternated from day to day. He also liked crackers and bread, cereal, berries, cherries, juice, lettuce, radish tops, and many of the greens. Sometimes he ate butter, cheese, sugar, salt, or milk. Occasionally, he ate ice cream. He and Rob both had great passions for chocolate milk shakes, and Rob could never get one past him; if Peep was anywhere in the vicinity, he came marching up purposefully to demand his share.

We often lunched in the family room, and at such times, Peep-Sight was sure to be there. He might fly up to a knee or a chair to peck at a candy bar or a piece of cake; he might put his foot on the rim of a glass and attempt to tip it down for a drink. He liked the cola drinks especially and even mastered drinking from a Coke bottle. He was inordinately fond of chocolate, sometimes eating a whole square, and he loved brownies.

Another of Peep's favorite foods was poppy seeds; he never tired of them. He would even abandon his native caution to stick his head into a small jar for them. When they were added to his regular seeds, the frequency of his pecking doubled or tripled instantly.

Peep was a neat and careful eater. He was especially fastidious about keeping his beak clean, and with messy foods, he would pause every few bites to wipe it with a sidewise whetting motion on whatever was handy. When he found a paper napkin on the kitchen counter, he appeared to use it for its intended purpose, but he often spoiled the impression by tearing off a strip and eating it. He liked to strip off pieces of Kleenex or newspaper as well and would down them with apparent relish. The cellulose presumably served him as roughage.

Peep had no rigid feeding schedule, but breakfast held a certain validity for him. As the sound of kitchen activities began in the morning, he gradually roused himself from the highboy in the dining room. After spending a little time in his flowerpot and putting himself in order, he would step off on a downward flight into the kitchen, buzzing in through the doorway and skidding to a halt on the counter. The smooth counter top was a little hard to negotiate at airborne speeds, so if his usual area wasn't clear when he came down, there could be trouble.

One morning Wanda had risen early to prepare a layer cake. Working in the kitchen, she stood back to admire the frosted cake. Suddenly and without warning, Peep came whirring in on his accustomed glide path and landed —Plop!—right in the middle of it. It was almost a rerun of the Peep-the-Sight episode.

It was hard to tell who was more surprised. There was Peep stuck to the cake, mushing about and getting covered with frosting as he tried to extricate himself; and there was Wanda, not sure whether she was annoyed or amused. Respecting his dignity, she stifled her laughter, plucked out the surprised bird, and took him to the sink. Once the incident had passed, however, she could no

longer control herself and the remembrance of his dodo-like arrival sent her into spasms of hilarity. For his part, Peep modified his flight plan for a few days thereafter to include a preliminary landing on the kitchen floor.

It was a long time before we realized that Peep wouldn't eat when he was alone. Upon our return from a weekend holiday, he greeted us briefly and then made his way at once to the feeder, apparently ravenous. After observing him behave this way consistently, we concluded that he did not eat at all during our absences. We then began to notice that even when we were home, he would almost invariably stop eating if we walked out on him, and he would resume when we returned. Apparently his instincts would simply not permit him to feed without someone standing guard.

Then one day Mike discovered that Peep sometimes fed alone in the lighted, empty kitchen at night. We guessed that his reflection in the dark, adjacent window pane satisfied his need for visible companionship. The reflection was not visible during the day because of the bright outdoors; but at night he could look up to see himself in a posture of alertness and thus be reassured. Normally, his reflection held little interest for him, so we concluded that this was instinctive behavior related to eating. Once we understood this, we left the kitchen light on and set a small mirror near his feeder when we were gone.

Although he still never bothered us at the dinner table, Peep was very fond of cocktail time. He probably enjoyed the socializing as much as the snacks—if there were guests, he was likely to be the center of attention. Cheese and crackers were a big favorite, and he would worry a salted peanut until someone crumbled it for him. After we had accepted the theory of his native judgment, we offered him whatever we had. He would try anything once, but he appeared to retain a permanent file of all previous rejects!

Most notable among these were the cocktails themselves, especially those made with gin. After the first trial, he would never even approach a martini again. (I envied him his good sense.) He did like some of the wines, however, and enjoyed a few drops of beer. If it was foamy, he would wipe his beak clean after each sip.

Generally Peep-Sight didn't like carbonated drinks; cola and root beer were the exceptions. Others he approached cautiously, then without sampling, he would shake his head, sneeze, or backpedal rapidly away with his head down and tail in the air.

Peep took such obvious delight in some foods, such as radish tops and poppy seeds, that I was always on the lookout for others that he might relish as much. In the supermarket, it took great restraint to pass the spice and herb racks without loading up on exotic condiments that I thought he might fancy. I didn't always make it. Sometimes I snitched little pieces of greens as I went through the produce department, secreting them in a shirt pocket or in a bag of carrots. When I got home I'd wash them off and call Peep to inspect and sample my loot. He was very choosy, however, and usually I forgot which was the endive and which was the rappini—the next time around, I'd have to start all over from scratch.

\*     \*     \*

Another activity that appeared frequently in my notes was the dust bath. This obviously has great importance for the bird, clearly affecting his health, grooming, hygiene, and general well-being. It serves many functions: to stimulate, to clean, and to buff the skin; to dislodge dander and vermin; and to brush the feathers. It might compare to our massage or rubdown, for it appears to be greatly refreshing and even restorative.

For this purpose, the flowerpot was all right to start the day, but it was not a satisfactory substitute for regular outdoor dust baths. These required one of us to be in attendance in order for him to feel secure enough to proceed. If the weather precluded our getting out for a day or two, Peep would fly back up to his flowerpot and begin kicking the contents about. We learned not to fill it too full, otherwise he'd strew dirt lightly about the dining room as he dusted.

The complex pattern of the dust bath must be instinctually transmitted too, for it was exhibited in all its basic elements from the start. In selecting an appropriate location, Peep-Sight looked for a relatively protected area near a shrub or rock. He would go from one side to another, pecking and scratching to test the texture and friability of the soil. Generally he liked fine, dry dust, although occasionally a cool, slight dampness was preferred. He improved his favorite spots with each use.

He began by pecking sharply in the earth and slashing sideways with his beak, thereby loosening the soil and dislodging pebbles or twigs. He scratched alternately with his feet and then resumed pecking. Continuing in this mode, he paused occasionally to replenish his gizzard with carefully selected bits of grit, and to savor whatever edibles he turned up in the process. Now and then he stopped to try out the shallow bowl he was making. Standing again, he'd work out the hard spots with his beak and feet. When the indentation became deeper, he began turning this way and that as he rubbed the sides and rounded them out with his body. Soon he was sitting in a nest of fine material. Then he began to work his feet and wings at the same time, expelling the dirt upward from under him on either side and simultaneously deflecting it onto his back with his wings. This marvelous display of coordination showered the natural talc through his raised feathers directly onto his skin. He continued to turn about as he worked, getting over on one wing or the other—sometimes almost flipping over onto his back. After a time, he would lie on his side and, pushing his feet against the rim of the bowl, force his back against the opposite side. This seemed to be especially pleasurable—he would close his eyes and stretch out his neck, apparently euphoric. Occasionally he turned his head over completely to rub his scalp into the dust.

Generally, a few moments of this completed the ritual. Standing up, he would shake a few times and whisk his tail rapidly from side to side. Then, with a satisfied cluck or two, he'd look about to get his bearings and go off to doze in the sun, settling down near someone who could be trusted to keep a sharp eye out for hawks.

\* \* \*

Finally, I found that many of my observations described Peep-Sight's sounds and calls. They were surprisingly different and distinct, although they merged easily into the bird sounds in the yard and the chatter of our other pets inside the house.

One of these pets was an intense, aristocratic Lutino parakeet named Golden Boy who had come to us about the same time as Peep-Sight. He was a bright canary yellow with a very fine frame and delicate feathers. An inscription banded to one leg suggested that he had hatched in California in 1965. Mike and Rob had come upon him, lost and near exhaustion, in a neighbor's yard. We could not find his owner and speculated that the bird had been lost for some time or had come from a considerable distance. He recovered quickly after his capture but remained completely wild and uncommunicative.

Golden Boy became a permanent part of our menagerie. Although he resisted Leslie's efforts at domestication, he slowly began to accommodate himself to being caged, and we discovered after a while that he had a talent for mimicking the wild birds outside. We moved him for a time to the family room, where he tolerated the clamor with evident disdain. Then one day we noticed him quietly practicing several of Peep-Sight's sounds. They were barely audible but quite passable. As he gained confidence his volume increased; soon he was able to deceive us at a distance.

The rest of us began imitating Peep, too. We borrowed directly from his vocabulary, finding that some approximation of his squawks or clucks was appropriate to certain circumstances. Chris became especially adept and sometimes appeared to converse with Peep in a simple way.

After a while, we came to appreciate the richness of the Gambel's language and to see that it was capable of communicating a wide variety of meaning. We probably understood only a fraction of it, but still we felt we knew something of what Peep-Sight was saying.

Frequently he used little sounds to keep in touch with us while he was occupied. Perhaps he was reminding us that he was distracted for the moment and shouldn't be counted upon to spot danger. When he was feeding, he made a distinctive throaty sound; when preening, he favored a single soft syllable. Sometimes he paced at a door or window, begging like a dog to go out—"Gerock, gerock, gerock." Once outside, however, he usually maintained "radio silence" unless he sighted potential danger.

Peep noted our comings and goings with a variety of chirps, clucks, and cheeps. If I had just stepped out for a moment, he'd acknowledge my return with a simple word; but if I had been gone longer, whether several hours or days, I was greeted with a casual effusion.

When entering upon a new encounter, Peep-Sight bobbed his head with jerky little movements and repeated in a tentative, evaluating tone, "Chip, chip, chip?" As he gradually became more committed, this changed to an argumentative: "Whit! Whit!" Finally he'd launch into a full-scale, loud, declarative blast: "Rio-RIT! Rio-RIT! Rio-RIT!"

A similar call with an important difference was his loud staccato "ROK-CHIK! ROK-CHIK! CHIK-CHIK!" Whereas the previous call was a specifically directed challenge, this one was an attention-directing alert: "What's going on out there? Who are those guys? Look what they're doing!"

One day I was in the backyard when I heard this call and looked up to see Peep-Sight at the kitchen window. He was obviously calling my attention to two boys who had just climbed onto the back wall. I turned and asked them to get off, and they promptly dropped from view. Peep persisted, however; so after a few minutes I let him out, assuming that he wanted to poke around in the yard or to take a dust bath. Instead he marched directly to the wall and flew up to where the boys had been. For several minutes he paced back and forth on the wall, scolding and threatening vigorously in the direction they had gone. In due time, satisfied that he'd lectured them properly, he dropped back down to the yard and went about his business—scratching in the flower beds and watching for hawks.

In the quail world, owls and hawks constitute a major threat. Peep's special alarms for danger from the air were readily recognizable as such. When he was outside, his eye was always on the sky and nothing that flew escaped his notice, whether it was a passing butterfly or a jet-liner six miles up. Here was an area in which we noticed his discrimination at work. Gradually he narrowed down his more urgent warnings to cover only the truly hawk-like objects, ignoring the sparrows and aircraft. The intensity of his warnings varied from a casual, throaty, "Gerp?" to a loud, urgent "GERP!" With the latter, he'd scrunch himself down as small as possible.

Peep used quite a different sound for potential danger on the ground. At the sight of any small furry animal (or even a far-fetched facsimile), he would make a string of percussive warning sounds: "Tuk-tuk-tuk-tuk-k. . . ." These started at a high frequency and intensity and gradually diminished as he investigated the strange object. He would approach it slowly, standing very tall and thin with his neck stretched up for maximum angle of observation. Then, as he checked out the intruder, the sound tapered off like a windup toy running down.

A dog or a cat would elicit this response—but so would the dust mop. The latter became his favorite domestic enemy, and he could detect its appearance instantly, even from another room. He always gave it the full treatment and could not relax completely until it was returned to the kitchen closet. Sometimes he just caught a glimpse of it under the door as he walked by, and he would acknowledge it with an offhand "Tuk-tuk" as he passed. Conditioning played its part here too, for eventually this signal came to have a stronger association with the dust mop than it did with the neighbor's cat!

In the wild, when a covey of quail takes flight, it ex-

plodes suddenly in all directions, and each individual emits a sharp, metallic "Kip-kip-kip-kip! . . ." The combined effect is a distracting clamor, startling and confusing to a potential predator. As the scattered birds coast back to the ground and take up new positions, their noises subside until just a single, occasional "Kip!" is heard thereafter. This assists the covey to reassemble. Several times Peep-Sight demonstrated this behavior when he became alarmed outdoors.

On rare occasions, Peep emitted a barely audible, high-pitched whistle. We thought this might be some special intimate communication. When Chris imitated it, Peep seemed to repeat it spontaneously and to become most attentive. We suspected it had to do with mating or constituted a secret warning. Since we didn't understand its importance, however, we generally refrained from using it.

The most familiar quail sounds, of course, are the calls. When Peep found himself unexpectedly alone, he would call out to see who was around. The basic call had considerable timbre: "Chuk-CAW?" After warming up with this once or twice, he began a regularized sequence: "Chuk-CAW, chuk-CAW, chuk-CAW, chuk-CAW-cay!" If we replied a few times (in our language or his), his calls soon subsided.

For a few weeks late each winter, Peep-Sight would stand on the back of a chair at the living room window, calling out in a special, mournful way. We assumed it was a signal for the re-pairing that begins in the wild about that time. His single loud "Caa-aaw?!" rose and fell plaintively, repeated four or five times per minute. In the quiet house, it sounded like the lonely call of someone long lost in the woods who is resigned and not really ex-

pecting an answer. One couldn't help feeling a little sad-
dened by it, and it was at these times especially that we
were likely to reopen the question of finding him a mate.

# 7

## A FEVER

In 1972, spring and summer came very early to southern Nevada. By mid-May the cushion chrysanthemums were fully grown and blooming in confusion; they normally bloom in fall. The season for winter annuals had been so brief that the Fish and Game Department was cautious about predicting the size of the quail population. We were even more cautious about undertaking an increase in our portion of it.

Surprisingly, the only factor that significantly affects the quail population from year to year is rainfall. Variations in temperature or the extent of the previous autumn's hunt are relatively unimportant compared to the character and amount of precipitation during the winter months.

This is not simply a matter of available water. The adaptable Gambel's quail is quite capable of surviving particularly arid periods. Raising healthy chicks is another matter, however, for they require tender vegetation and insects in abundance. When it looks as though it will be a lean year, nature in her compassionate way attempts to limit the number of progeny produced so that few will go hungry.

The key is in the "winter annuals," the freshly germinating seeds and sprouts that appear in winter months under good conditions. They are rich in vitamin E, which is critical to quail fertility. The winter annuals require soaking winter rains; without a good period of feeding on them, the quail experience many nesting failures and small clutches. Hence, the size of the quail hatch for the following year can be predicted with some confidence by observing the number and timing of the slow fine drizzles that come during mid-winter.

It was unclear whether 1972 was going to be a good year for quail or not. While there had been rains, the early arrival of warm weather had cut short the winter growing season, and the prognosis was uncertain.

However, it was summer, and before long it would be time to make a decision. If a mate for Peep was a prospect this year, action had to be taken soon. As usual, we took turns arguing the pros and cons. On the one hand, chances of success were not great; and yet if we made it, it could mean buying into a lot of trouble! Nevertheless, worthwhile experiences come when one is willing to accept some risk.

A new plan was proposed. We would obtain one female chick from the stock of our breeder friend as soon as we could be sure of its gender. We would attempt to raise her in the house as we had done with Peep-Sight. Everything then would ride on this one effort. Without those first few weeks, could she possibly be tamed?

We couldn't agree that the plan was good enough to

implement, but I did call the breeder to check on the availability of his stock. He was expecting only two small hatches of Gambel's quail about a week apart. I called him twice more in the next three weeks. Then finally, the first chicks had hatched. Still we were undecided.

*   *   *

One Saturday morning I had been out cleaning the pool and enjoying the sun and, as I came in to lunch, I noticed that the house was uncharacteristically quiet. The younger boys were there, and I should have heard Peep's usual racket. Where was his customary counterpoint to their inevitable clamor?

I went investigating and discovered him fluffed out on the floor of the family room, facing toward the wall. His eyes were closed and his breathing rapid. No one remembered noticing anything untoward, but we all agreed now that his appearance was not normal.

He seemed to be seeking seclusion; so after consulting a moment, we moved him to another corner of the room where we devised a little shelter of two chairs and a cushion with a blanket draped over the top.

It soon became clear that he was very ill. He could barely hold up his head, and when forced to move, literally crawled on his belly. At a complete loss for an explanation, we thought of pneumonia or a stroke. Possibly his uncanny intuition had finally failed to warn him of some new insecticide on the lettuce. With a sinking feeling we recalled reading about Newcastle disease, a bird killer that had been reported closing in from Arizona and California.

We considered calling a veterinarian, but we had no current relationship with one, nor did we know of any who specialized in birds. Besides, moving him looked much too risky, and a house call was unheard of.

For the next several hours, Peep sat in a lifeless little

huddle. He was so completely motionless we could only check on his breathing, which was erratic—sometimes labored, sometimes shallow. He seemed to become weaker and weaker, and eventually he lay completely prostrate with his neck outstretched and his face buried pathetically in the carpet.

Our experience with sick birds was that they almost never recovered, and none of us recalled one as sick as this. Very glum, we kept reminding one another how lucky we were to have had him with us for three years.

He lingered on. We offered water, but he was unresponsive. Leslie warmed some sugared milk with several drops of bourbon and administered it with an eyedropper. Peep worked his beak feebly and seemed appreciative, but his condition did not improve. Searching about for something to do, I resurrected the old cigar box with its Christmas tree lights and covered it with a sock, just as we had done in devising his brooder that first night several years before. I placed it next to him, and its radiant warmth appeared to comfort him. Eventually we retired, but during the night, one or another of us was up every hour or so to check on his condition.

Amazingly, he persevered and gradually began holding his head up in its normal position. By the next morning, he looked decidedly better and accepted some sugar water. Later he took a few halting steps. When he pecked at some grit, we began to take hope, even though each new effort obviously exhausted him and had to be followed by a lengthy nap.

In the afternoon he came to the middle of the room for a short time, moving very slowly. Between frequent rest periods he grew more active, eating a few poppy seeds, drinking water, and even chip-ing feebly at the boys as they passed his way. By evening he had fluttered up to the coffee table, and at bedtime he was looking for his regular roost on the highboy!

I lifted him up to it, and he spent a restful night. The next morning he flew down without apparent difficulty. During the day, still resting frequently, he gradually recouped his strength; by evening he was eating at the feeder almost like old times. When I offered the open jar of poppy seeds, he stuck his head in and ravenously gulped them by the beakful. Of course he had lost weight, and we noticed that he favored his left foot, but it too seemed to strengthen as his general health improved. On the fourth morning of his illness, he went outside for a convalescent dust bath, and by afternoon his level of activity was almost normal.

To us, it seemed like a miracle. In the short space of only a few days, the feisty little fellow had become suddenly ill and had made a remarkable recovery. In our somewhat superstitious way, we took his reprieve as a sign. We decided to make another call to the game breeder.

\* \* \*

There was still one detail to be faced. I had always been uneasy about the legal aspects of our keeping Peep-Sight. The state of Nevada, I felt quite sure, had numerous regulations regarding captive wildlife. Undoubtedly these would turn out to be well-taken and protective in intent; but still, their implementation could prove awkward for us. An insensitive official taking his job too seriously might demand that Peep, despite his three years of domestic life, be returned to the desert. Of course I should have to refuse, and I envisioned one of those ridiculous court battles over custody—the natural versus the adopted parents, etc. . . . It seemed better to avoid the whole uncomfortable situation and not to attract official attention unnecessarily.

Now, however, with the prospect of deliberately adding to our brood, I felt it best to face the issue.

As I walked into the Fish and Game Department, a number of uniformed officials were occupied casually at their desks. The center of activity, however, was obviously the matronly woman who sat behind the counter, wielding the telephone with deadly bureaucratic skill. As I waited for her to finish her call, my eyes wandered around the room.

There was the infamous walking catfish that had been

captured in the nick of time (and pickled in formalde-
hyde) before he could terrorize Lake Mead. There was
the inevitable mountain sheep, apparently sticking its
head through the wall from the adjacent room, staring
glass-eyed off into the distance. And there in a brightly
illuminated cabinet were a pair of Gambel's quail, dry
and lifeless, but posed paradoxically in positions of attention. Before I could examine my feelings, I was being ad-
dressed:

"May I help you?"

"Oh, yes. I wanted to see about getting a permit to
keep some quail."

"Gambel's? What sort of permit do you want?"

"Well, I don't know. I was just going to, you know,
*raise* them, and . . ."

"Do you plan to sell any?"

"Oh, no. Actually, they will be pets."

It turned out that I needed a Hobby Permit—Non-
Commercial Breeding Ground—two dollars per year. She
cautioned me that I was not allowed to take money for
them, but I could give them away or eat them myself (I
gulped!).

When she asked where I planned to get the quail, I
named my breeder friend and she nodded her approval.
At this, I became emboldened and confessed, "As a matter of fact, we already have one of them. My boy found it
as a baby chick in the desert. . . ."

She frowned; I knew I had made a mistake. I suffered
through a brief lecture about permitting my children to
remove wildlife from the wild, then gave her the money
and pertinent information, and received my license in return. As I took it in my hand, a comfortable feeling of le-

gitimacy settled over me. I thanked her and started out, but she called after to remind me once more: "Be sure you don't sell any. You may give them away, or . . ."

Driving home, I found myself wondering what *she* might think about cherry pie filling.

# 8

## LADY BIRD

I suppose her name was inevitable. At first of course, she had no name at all, and so we merely referred to her as *the* lady bird. Soon we were dropping the *the* and beginning to say it in such a way that you could *hear* the initial capitals. Before long, like it or not, there it was: Lady Bird.

As a name, it was more hopeful than appropriate. It certainly didn't fit the tattered little ragamuffin I first brought home. Pacing about in the small cage that we had used for transporting lizards, she looked somewhat the worse for wear.

She was only a few weeks old but feathered out in the characteristic mottled beige. Her feet were predictably large, and to us, she seemed generally out of proportion. Furthermore, her tail feathers were broken and her plumes bedraggled. But nothing in her manner suggested that *she* had any concern about her ridiculous appearance.

She was completely wild. This was hardly surprising, as a game breeder is likely to avoid domesticating influences on his birds. They are generally destined to take their place eventually in nature, and any accommodation to civilization or the presence of humans would only interfere with their ultimate adaptation to the native environment.

Nonetheless, we were not quite prepared for her to be so totally alien and unreachable. After living with Peep, we found it hard to accept her obvious concept of us as hostile, even predatory. The contrast between the two birds was extreme, and I was reminded of a dog we had when I was a boy.

She was a marvelously intelligent retriever named Cobina, a hunting dog, but part of the family. In some mysterious way, she always seemed to fathom what we were saying and to respond with appropriate behavior. Our rapport was remarkable. When she was nearly six years old, Cobina developed a brain tumor; and after that, the pressure of excitement would suddenly destroy her recognition of everything familiar, temporarily cutting her off from us. In an instant she was a wild thing, viewing us all with suspicion and distrust, and no amount of coaxing or cajoling could establish our amiable intent. Eventually she would relax, and things would snap back into place; she returned to us as though from an absence, tail-wagging and communicative.

Our contact with Peep-Sight had been so close and trusting that the drastically opposite reaction of the unapproachable little chick was a shock, like those first bewildering episodes long ago with Cobina and her tumor.

We agreed not to bring Lady Bird to Peep-Sight's attention just yet—not only for quarantine purposes, but also to let her calm down.

In preparing for the new chick, we had thought again of the meany-olium. It had not been put to use since we moved, and now the boys expended a lot of effort in sealing the cracks and hauling in bushels of fine, clean blow sand. This came over the back wall, one canful at a time, to provide a good base and ample dust-bathing facilities. Ultimately, however, we decided once more against it. It could only delay the process of getting her used to us and to the house.

Instead, her little cage was placed in the family room at one end of the elevated hearth. I put blow sand inside and

provided seeds and water. The back and one end were protected, and in the evenings, the cage was covered completely.

At first she mostly paced and peeped; she tripped and spilled the water and behaved like any captured wild baby animal. From time to time, she settled down to rest and seemed reasonably comfortable; but whenever we came too near, she was up and agitated.

In a few days she appeared to accept the situation. We would notice her scratching for food or taking a furtive drink, or taking a hurried, surreptitious dust bath. Once or twice when replenishing food and water, I captured her, holding her for a moment and talking softly. It had scant effect; for the most part she might as well have been a fledgling sparrow fallen from its nest.

Eventually Peep-Sight noticed the activity at the hearth and walked over casually to investigate. Lady Bird became rather excited, trying to attract his attention both by her calls and by her actions. His interest was short-lived, however, and he strolled away, apparently writing her off as just another parakeet or canary.

\* \* \*

One evening Lady Bird managed to get loose. Since Peep was in another part of the house, we took the opportunity to see how she would behave outside the cage. Leslie positioned herself to block off the only exit from the family room, while Wanda and I simply kept to our chairs. Lady Bird scurried about the room, taking advantage of the furniture for cover. After the initial impact of new-found freedom, she became curious and investigated every corner. Occasionally she stopped to pick at something in the carpet or to look around and take stock of her surroundings. We talked to her and moved around a bit, letting her get used to things. She could fly well when she chose to, but she generally kept to the floor. After a while we captured her and returned her to the cage.

The next night we repeated the exercise with more of the family involved. It became a regular occurrence; she obviously enjoyed it and appeared to chafe at being returned to the cage. Then, getting by the guard at the door one night, she took to exploring the rest of the house, and thereafter it became more difficult to recapture her.

About a week later, I replaced the little carrying cage with a larger, roomier one in the same familiar location on the hearth. It had a removable pan for blow sand on the bottom, and better facilities for seeds and water. A door opened out and down at one end, and at the opposite end, I installed Peep's former Christmas-light cigar box covered with a sock.

It was a tremendous immediate success, and her level of self-assurance seemed to improve at once. Since the new cage had considerable height, I was able to provide a protected perch. It was close enough to be warmed by the Christmas lights, and she loved to sit there and nap securely in the daytime. At night she went up to roost as soon as the cage was covered.

Eventually she found even the larger cage confining, so we began leaving the door open, enabling her to come and go as she liked. Soon she was spending most of the day outside the cage; at night, we'd capture her and enclose her in it. When the cage was uncovered in the morning, she would immediately fly against the door, making a great ruckus to get out.

*    *    *

Then one night she couldn't be found. We gave up finally, knowing she was lurking about somewhere, hiding behind the cabinets or the sofa. The next morning, there she was feeding at the cage, but as soon as I walked in, she darted away and out of sight. It appeared that she had enjoyed and appreciated the cage but didn't want to be locked into it anymore.

Soon a new pattern was established with Lady Bird living free in the family room, although keeping under cover and invisible most of the time. The cage was removed but its features were retained—food and water and a change of dust—at the same location on the hearth. The sheltered perch stayed too, and she continued to use it. She clearly viewed it as home base, but when taken by surprise, she scurried away. Sometimes we laughingly called her "the Gray Ghost," for she seemed to materialize from nowhere or to blur peripherally across the room.

Gradually the little bird became less spooked by us, until finally we might walk in carefully and not send her hurrying off. Then if one sat relatively still, she would move freely about. Now when we sat in the family room with our snacks, sometimes she would appear quietly and forage for scraps.

One afternoon Wanda sat on the sofa with a small plate of hors d'oeuvres as I sat reading across the room. Silently, Lady Bird emerged from behind the cabinets and started inching her way along the opposite end of the couch from Wanda. Then she flew up to the arm and, after looking carefully about, began edging cautiously along the back. Wanda was aware of her but did not pay much attention. Suddenly Lady Bird charged down to the plate, snatched up a large piece of dried beef as she passed, and raced rapidly away, tripping and falling and finally careening to safety behind a chair!

She was as hilarious and yet pathetic in her deceptiveness as the hungry homeless waif in the silent movies, stealing a loaf of bread and darting off to the abandoned tenement. We decided that she might need a change of diet and discovered that meal worms would not only draw her out of hiding, but would also induce her to eat from our hands. However, she had to compete with Peep-Sight

for these, and it took a little special effort to be sure she got a share.

At this time, Lady Bird had been with us only two or three weeks, and we felt it was not too late to abandon the experiment if that appeared desirable. The time was approaching, however, when it would be difficult to return her to a wild state without ill effect. A family conference was in order before proceeding further.

We reviewed how well the taming process seemed to be going and tested one another's optimism. Should we continue or should we return the little chick to the game breeder while it was still feasible to do so?

It was clear that Peep was totally disinterested in our decision. As he saw it, Lady Bird was just an animated toy or another of our nonintelligent pets.

We agreed finally to continue with the effort, at least for a little while, and before long, Peep-Sight found it difficult to maintain his indifference.

# 9

## ADOLESCENCE REVISITED

As Lady Bird became less frightened of us, she began showing a special interest in Peep. Seeing him resting near our feet, she would approach and sit near him. He might look up, a little annoyed, but when nothing happened, she'd move in closer until she was right up against him. He would then move off a little way to maintain his aplomb, but she soon followed to try again.

At first when she approached, she actually leaned against him so that as he stepped indignantly away, she fell over. If he were dozing on one foot, she might come up to him so vigorously as to topple him over instead. Then she got a peck on the head for her exuberance!

Lady Bird became such a pest that Peep began flying up to a chair or a table to get away from her, but before long, she was following him there. Then he took to sitting next to one of us or on a knee, relying on her reticence to keep her away. This worked for a day or two, but we were on her side, and soon she was bold enough to follow him there too. Then I could come in and find Mike watching television, legs stretched out in front, one bird comfortably ensconced on each knee!

Sometimes when Lady Bird was dogging him, Peep-Sight would suddenly dart back and forth a few times or fly up to the traverse rods. But she would simply model his evasive behavior, darting or flying along with him.

Seeing Peep around so close to all of us, Lady Bird was encouraged to join in the group. As long as he was near, she felt safe; when he was not in the room, she stayed mostly to the protected nooks behind the sofa or cabinets. After a while the two of them would sometimes settle down and form a little covey with our feet as we sat. Perhaps Lady Bird would snuggle up to my foot instead of to Peep-Sight, finding it more tolerant of her pushing. I could then reach down to pick her up, but I had to be very devious about it. At my first stirring, she'd become alert and dash off across the room. After a while, she became easier to catch and didn't struggle at being held. Her heart would palpitate for a moment or two, but I would rub her head gently and talk soothingly to her; soon she was comfortably asleep, enjoying the warmth. After I had turned out the lights in the evening, I could place her on the perch where she'd stay all night.

Peep-Sight had no reservations about helping himself to food and water at Lady Bird's home base on the hearth, but she was reluctant to join him at his feeder on the kitchen counter. It was too open and exposed for her sense of security. For a time this provided him a last respite from her tagging along.

Peep continued to respond rather unfavorably to Lady Bird's advances. His spectrum of reactions went from reluctant tolerance to aggravated rejection. In nature, the Gambel's roosters are quite devoted to the upbringing of the young, and should the mother disappear, will even substitute for her. Apparently, however, their instincts do not contemplate thrusting a half-grown orphan upon a confirmed, crusty, old bachelor!

\* \* \*

As she reached adolescence, Lady Bird became uproariously awkward. Although she could zip about with great alacrity, she waddled like a duck when she walked. Her legs angled outward and her large feet spraddled. Even so, she stepped on them frequently.

Sometimes after a nap, she would stand and stretch out one wing and a foot, and then fall over on her side! Scratching the back of her head she often knocked herself over. She even showed a lack of coordination when preening, burying her head in her tail feathers only to lose her balance and topple backwards.

Her tail feathers were always bent and broken, and she was generally in disarray. Her topknot consisted of two valiant plumes held back at an angle, one curving forward to the left and the other, somewhat shorter, forward and to the right. The resulting effect of antennae made her look like some scrawny ridiculous insect, and I found myself calling her Lady *Bug*.

While we remembered Beau Peep as resembling Tweetie Bird of the Warner Brothers' cartoons, Lady Bird was a living version of Snoopy's little friend Woodstock with his frazzled feathers and his knocking about. Even when she flew, she struggled and bumbled along, banging into things and sliding to a landing, just as he did.

Somehow through all the ludicrous antics and demeanor came an undeniable charm. Here was the sober, pathetic little hobo-clown; she made you laugh while she stole your heart.

*    *    *

Lady Bird learned a version of the primary quail call, and we often heard her "Chuck-CAW" in a high, thin voice when she was looking for Peep. Of course he ignored her. Chances are he had sneaked off to get away from her in the first place.

He seemed to be increasingly annoyed by her persis-

tence in following him about and pushing against him. Finally he resorted to pecking her hard on the head or to taking a tug at her less than handsome tail feathers. Even this was not effective, for she'd just scrunch down, close her eyes, and hang in doggedly. Apparently she was willing to pay this price for his company. We were concerned that he might injure her, but fortunately he never cut the skin.

Eventually she got the message and found that he would tolerate her if she didn't insist on jamming up so close. When she first approached him, she still got a perfunctory peck or two, but then he would permit her to settle in next to him, not quite touching. A *rapprochement* was developing.

Surprisingly, Peep-Sight appeared to have no objection when Lady Bird finally did begin joining him at his feeder. Basically a social activity, feeding was apparently not included among his jealously guarded bachelor prerogatives. In fact, while Lady Bird never actually stood guard, her presence seemed to satisfy Peep's instinctive need for a sentry, for now we found they would eat together in our absence.

Of course, by Peep's standards, Lady Bird was a little lacking in the social graces. She was likely to perch on the jigger of juice as he drank or to wade right into the cereal bowl from which he sipped punctiliously. Furthermore, it was not even beyond her ethic to snatch a raspberry from under his very beak!

On the other hand, it was the venturesome Lady Bird who discovered the toaster, to their mutual delight. Access to that side of the counter required negotiating a precariously narrow walkway along the front edge of the sinks, and Peep-Sight had never attempted it. Apparently attracted by the reflectant chrome, the indomitable Lady Bird merely wobbled fearlessly across, and once there, discovered a selection of tasty, toasted crumbs. This brought Peep edging over cautiously like a tight-rope walker, and thus they had added new variety to their breakfast fare.

Lady Bird simply could not keep our late hours, and when we were in the family room, her perch on the hearth was not suitable for serious sleeping—there was too much noise and light. So, early in the evening, she would unobtrusively disappear. Upon retiring, we'd spot her in the darkened living room, roosting atop a bookshelf or on the curtain rods. Sometimes I would put her back on the

hearth perch after the lights were out, but often I simply left her. In the morning she'd be at the sunny window watching the outside activities before Peep was even awake.

While Peep-Sight accepted Lady Bird at his feeder, his roost atop the highboy and the sanctity of his flowerpot were another matter altogether. One day when he was on the highboy, Lady Bird flew up to join him, and it was soon clear that this time she had gone too far. He stalked her from one side to the other, pecking her repeatedly, and even though she huddled up as small as possible at an extreme corner, he sneaked around the flowerpot to punish her again. After each peck, he would retreat righteously, then looking back and seeing her still there, he would return to repeat the process. Finally I reached up and rescued her, advising her to abandon that particular goal for the time being.

She did need a regular roosting spot, however, and began using a stack of books on the uppermost shelf in the living room. These were at a height and position remarkably similar to Peep's roost on the highboy. It was a little hard on the books, but it did have possibilities, and I began to think about it.

But first, it was time once more to take stock of where we were and where we were going. After due consideration, we again decided to continue. This time we felt truly committed to the plan; we were going to make it work if we could. It was clear that Peep-Sight wasn't won over, but the rest of us were.

# 10

## MOMENT OF TRUTH

In a household as boisterous and active as ours, Lady Bird was probably prudent to be cautious. Nonetheless, she continued to adapt and to be more at home with us, and we were encouraged. She didn't seem to mind when I turned off the Christmas lights; she began to nap in other locations.

At night she continued to use her roost on the bookshelf. Early in the evening she would slip away, and when I checked the house before retiring, there she would be, nestled comfortably on *Run to Daylight* and leaning against *The Peoples of Kenya*. We were pleased that she had found a place of her own, but we weren't entirely satisfied with it. Then I had an inspiration.

I bought an attractive flowerpot, not quite as large as Peep's, and filled it partially with sand to weight it down. Then I cut a piece of hardware mesh and formed it into a shallow bowl, installing it in the flowerpot to provide a false bottom only an inch or two down. Finally I put in the old reliable sock to make a soft nest. If she accepted the arrangement, I planned to remove the sock and rely on the hardware mesh to support her comfortably while permitting her droppings to pass through.

I placed the flowerpot on the high shelf next to the books, close enough so the little bird could easily hop over to it if she chose. Its height was just a little below that of the books and its appearance was quite acceptable, even to Wanda.

That night, when Lady Bird disappeared from the family room, I tiptoed in to check. She was roosting in her usual spot on the books. In an hour or so I returned, and there she was as snug as could be, comfortably settled in her very own flowerpot! After that, when she retired she went directly to her little nest and ignored the books entirely.

*   *   *

As time passed, our two birds seemed to be working out a relationship. Eventually it took only one or two token pecks for Peep to moderate a situation to his satisfaction. Actually there was clear accommodation on both sides. He was much more tolerant of her tagging after him, and she was a lot less persistent in doing so. She began to establish some favorite spots of her own and often seemed quite content by herself without calling and searching for him. In the morning they took up complementary positions on the backs of the two chairs at the living room window, enjoying the morning sun, seeing the neighborhood off to school, and occcasionally exchanging comments. Only infrequently now would she sidle up to him, pushing him off balance and getting a peck on the head for it.

Lady Bird took to sleeping much of the day in the family room, under the end table next to the couch. Sitting there, as long as I didn't move too fast, I could put my hand down next to her and stroke her with one finger. A gross movement, however, would still send her scurrying away.

When one of us sat in the big chair, she'd sometimes surprise us by flying up unexpectedly to the arm to see if we had anything to eat. Often we did, and she'd dig right in and help herself, tugging at a piece of ham until her feet slipped out from under her, or running off happily with a stolen chunk of cheese.

We soon found we could call her out of hiding by imitating her soft "two-eet, two-eet" to offer her some treat. Her tastes, too, were eclectic, but they were different from Peep's. For example, she liked the processed meats that Peep never ate; but she had no interest at all in his favorites, chocolate or Coke. Furthermore, poppy seeds and cherry pie filling were nothing special to her either. They agreed on greens, however, and she could devour a remarkable quantity of boiled broccoli.

We were anxious to get Lady Bird outside, for we were sure there were things she needed that just weren't available indoors. Still, we were afraid that it wasn't safe. She was pretty skittish yet, and even with Peep-Sight there to reassure her or to call her back, we thought it risky. Cats and small dogs continued to surprise us occasionally in the backyard, and the street was just over the wall.

One day while Wanda sat with Peep as he dust bathed, I carried Lady Bird just outside the door and set her down on the patio. I brought along some meal worms to distract her, and she seemed reassured by my presence. It was clear that she was fascinated by the strange new surroundings, but she was also very cautious and didn't move far away. She appeared to appreciate the outing, but when I opened the door to the family room, she was eager to return to the familiarity of her home.

We took her out again the next day, and soon she was exploring the flower beds with Peep-Sight and enjoying outdoor dust baths. We continued to guard both birds

carefully, remembering how long it had taken to clearly establish boundaries for Peep, and how easily he had been spooked.

\* \* \*

Lady Bird and Peep were increasingly comfortable together—they were not close, but they were together. Although each appeared to like being alone, they often napped near each other and fed together or watched out the same window. Sometimes they seemed to call one another from separate parts of the house. It began to look as though our farfetched plan just might work after all.

Lady Bird was growing; she had already reached the "little turkey" stage, and we were eager for her to mature. We were not sure how old she was but felt that in only a few more weeks she would be fully grown.

She began moulting quite heavily, in what we thought might be the change to her adult plumage. Moulting can be an especially difficult time for birds; they often become ill or mopey and require a special diet. Peep-Sight had always managed quite well, but Leslie's parakeets frequently had a bad time.

One evening Lady Bird failed to go to her roost, and we couldn't find her until the next day; she was hiding under one of the boys' beds. Clearly not herself, she got no better as the day passed. When we took her out to the flower beds she perked up some, but was obviously exhausted upon her return.

Soon she was huddled under the end table, obviously indisposed. We brought out the Christmas lights and a jigger of sugar water, and provided a little shelter for her, but all to no avail. We did our best to make her comfortable, but we could not do enough. She closed her eyes and lay quite still, and sometime during the night, the little gray ghost gave up.

# 11

## REPRISE

Peep-Sight did not pine for Lady Bird, nor did he appear to be greatly distraught by her disappearance. Certainly there had been no strong bond established between them in the short time of their modest rapport. In fact, had her demise come a month earlier, he might have been relieved to be rid of the annoyance. Occasionally he seemed to be casually looking for her; he came frequently to the hearth where her feeder and dust bath had been. Possibly he was only checking for leftover seeds.

I suspect we missed her more than he. For several weeks as we sat in the family room, we thought we glimpsed the little chick in our peripheral vision, darting from under a chair to the back of the cabinets. Sometimes we imagined that we heard her quiet little chirps coming from behind the couch.

She had provided a study in contrasts. There was her raggedy appearance and frenetic movements versus Peep's majestic elegance and calm aplomb. Then too, though she was always so sober and intense, her actions were comic and awkward. Finally there was her insistence on dogging Peep-Sight and snuggling up to him, even though it meant taking a lot of punishment in return.

She had been a charming little creature, though in quite a different way from Beau Peep. We had anxiously anticipated her transformation into poised adult beauty and were sorry to have been deprived of it. While the coloration of the female Gambel's quail is more subdued than that of the male, we felt sure that it was fully as handsome, and we had looked forward to the same leisurely appreciation of it that had so delighted us in Peep's first year. Her name would have fitted her eventually, we were sure.

We never regretted undertaking the experiment. It is unlikely that Lady Bird's chances for survival were diminished by our adopting her, and for us, it was truly a worthwhile experience. It had been valuable for its own sake, but also for what it had taught us about raising quail. We had no specific plans for the moment, but after all, we were registered now with the Nevada Department of Fish and Game as non-commercial breeders. Who knows what we might attempt next year?

*     *     *

The combined effect of Peep's illness and our experience with Lady Bird made us all that much more appreciative of what we had. We began keeping a better eye on him and on his general condition, and we no longer took his robust health for granted.

One evening I noticed him working vigorously at his

left foot. Both feet had a few elongated scales that grew straight out, and we had conjectured that there might be mites under them. The left one was especially bad, and I remembered that he had favored it noticeably at the time of his first serious illness.

Sure enough, the next day he was obviously sick again, although not so severely as before. This time it lasted for about a week, and we were especially careful that he got variety in his diet, plenty of rest, and not too much activity. Once again, he favored the left foot strongly; for a time he refused to use it at all.

Gradually he got better and returned to normal in all respects, except possibly slowed down just a little. We determined to get some expert advice. A quail's life expectancy, after all, is said to be about three to five years, and he was already in that range. If he had a mite infestation, it would probably continue to take its toll, and one of these times his reserve of strength might not be adequate to the occasion.

Taking him out to the vet wouldn't be a simple matter. He hadn't even been in the car for several years, and if he became frightened by the traffic or flew about as I drove, it could be hazardous. But we no longer had a cage, and in any case, that would probably just frighten him more. Once inside a veterinarian's office it could be worse, especially in the waiting room. With a variety of cats and dogs all about, I would have to confine him carefully in my hands. Even in an examining room, he might not remain still long enough to be examined!

I made some inquiries and got the name of a vet who had a reputation for birds. I explained the problem briefly on the phone, and then later talked with him in his office.

I agreed to try one of the commercial miticides first. When this didn't seem to help, we decided to take Peep in.

Wanda held him as we started out in the car, but he soon appeared to be fairly at ease so she let him stand on the dash as I drove. He was alert and interested, watching all the strange sights and commenting excitedly at the rapidly passing cars and buildings.

We were able to park near the entrance to the office, and I went in first to make arrangements and clear the way. I felt like the Secret Service arranging for a presidential visit! Waiting to register, I could look out through a side door and see Peep-Sight in the window of our Pinto, remarking loudly (ROK-CHIK!) at each Persian or poodle that paraded by.

When our turn came, I brought Peep in through the side entrance to a small examining room, barren except for a stainless steel table and a lavatory. Wanda set him on the table and he was quite at home, alert but not frightened. When the doctor slipped in and spoke to him softly, Peep merely gave him the "unknown visitor" treatment, and even permitted him to take scrapings without serious objection. Microscopic inspection confirmed mite-infestation, and the doctor provided a lotion to cure it.

The trip home was accomplished without difficulty. Peep-Sight seemed to have enjoyed the adventure so much that we resolved to take him for a ride again sometime soon.

The lotion appeared to work. The material under the scales dislodged, the infected scales sloughed off, and Peep showed no further special concern for them. We were relieved.

A few weeks later, Wanda and I drove him out to an isolated bit of desert and walked around with him in the dunes and mesquite. He took several dust baths and thoroughly explored a huge briar patch, flushing out a surprised cottontail. He found a number of exotic edibles that were no longer available in his own landscaped yard and generally had a good outing. When we returned home, he settled in immediately on top of the television with his head under his wing, resting up from all the fresh air and exercise.

\* \* \*

Another Christmas came, and as usual, Peep delighted in the placing of the tree and the stringing of the lights. As soon as it was in its stand, he flew up into the branches to help. By the time the trimming began, he was off on the arm of a chair, resting and watching. I had just completed my studies at the university, and the family was all home together, although of course our interests were increasingly divergent as the children grew older. Peep-Sight appreciated the festivities as much as anyone.

As spring came in 1973, Peep-Sight began showing his age. He became even less tolerant with visitors, as well as with Mike and Rob. Then, more seriously, he began sometimes to ignore them, apparently too tired to scold. Despite our presumed success with eliminating the mites from his feet, he continued to fall ill occasionally, and each time upon recovery, seemed to have slowed down just a little.

I was back at work now, and I think he missed our mornings of study. Sometimes as I was getting ready for a day at the office, he would come in and take his position at the desk, as though inviting me to stay home and keep him company. Often I wished I could.

It seemed as though he slept with his head under a wing more frequently. Many days he simply remained on top of the highboy until everyone had left, dozing next to the flowerpot after his morning "shower." Apparently, once the house was empty, he flew down and napped under the table, skipping breakfast until I came home at noon. He seemed reluctant to eat unless I was personally standing guard for him, and often I had to coax him to be sure he was getting enough.

In cool weather it took special encouragement to get him outside for his dust bath, and he was likely to hurry through it cursorily. He began spending less time at his preening, and eventually even his movements suggested a certain stiffness.

Finally there was no escaping it: Peep-Sight had lived to be an old bird. Perhaps it was just as well that Lady Bird had not survived, for she might have been disappointed in him! On the other hand, while he was not as feisty, confident, and well-groomed as he had been, he was still charming and perhaps more companionable than before. Where he had been scolding and officious, he was now merely mildly grumpy. He enjoyed the hearth, and when I sat in my favorite chair in the evenings, he began coming regularly to sit next to me, always to my left and in the same spot on the cushion. In many ways he was just comfortable and mellow, like a faithful old dog.

It was nearly four years since that May day when Mike had come bursting out into the backyard with a little ball of down cupped in his grimy hands, excited about finding a baby bird, yet not quite realizing what he had. In many ways four years is quite a long time. For a quail, it is fifteen times longer than it takes him to grow into maturity. And yet that first three months after hatch-out must itself be a marvelously rich, full period, for in that short time he discovers and subdues a whole, exciting world.

For the rest of us, many things had changed in four years. Mike was nearly thirteen now; Leslie was eighteen and engaged. Outside near a different pool, a new set of palm trees was challenging me to tackle last year's barbed fronds. Over the back wall we could still see the calico-colored mountains, but often now they were obscured by a brown smudge. On the Strip, MGM's new Grand Hotel was pushing up and out, striving to rob the Dunes of its eminence. Howard Hughes was thrice removed, and Frank Sinatra was actually in retirement.

It was an unusual year, 1973. In the first few months, the Las Vegas area had already received its total average

annual precipitation, and it had all come in well-spaced, slow, soaking rains. The desert was responding with its most luxurious growth in fifteen years; some said in fifty. Soon there would be blooms everywhere, incredibly profuse: wild poppies and verbena, thistle, forget-me-nots, Indian paintbrush, lupines, cane cactus, and prickly pears. Slopes that had been brown for years would suddenly turn green, and the area would come alive with birds, lizards, and insects.

Undeniably, southern Nevada residents were due for a very special year. It would be a good spring to start a lawn; it would be a splendid summer for water sports on Lake Mead; it would be an outstanding season for growing roses and day lilies.

And this time there could be no doubt: it was going to be an especially good year for the desert quail.

# EPILOGUE

Peep-Sight's sense of timing and his flair for the dramatic did not fail him, even at the end. I had been most anxious to complete the writing of his tale while he was still alive; it would be more difficult once he was gone. Working on the last chapters I felt a sense of urgency, for his health was ebbing. It seemed as though he understood and was hanging on until I could finish.

Finally, on a sunny Saturday afternoon I had written the ending, and with only Mike and myself at hand, Peep called it quits. Characteristically, he had chosen his moment, maintaining his poise and dignity to the last. He left just as he had come—on his own terms.

We miss him of course. When we were a family growing up, Peep-Sight was one of us, and in his unique way he helped to make those special years that much more special. The pleasure and insight he provided can never be lost; they are an inseparable part of the times we had together.

# APPENDIX

# GENERAL OBSERVATIONS
# ON GAMBEL'S QUAIL

When Peep-Sight arrived on the scene, we were almost totally unfamiliar with the ways of the Gambel's quail, but his four years in our family changed all that. We took every opportunity to observe the "real quail," comparing their natural behavior to Peep's domestic antics, and to exchange observations with others who were interested. A few of our contacts—the breeder, the ranger, the veterinarian—had broad experience to draw upon, and with them we would discuss the subject at length. We discovered that the *Outdoors* writer for our local newspaper[3] was himself a devoted quail-watcher. And then there was Mr. Gorsuch's valuable research from 1934, which filled in many of the blanks. In due course we had noted and compared, hypothesized and tested, until we found we

---

[3]Ray Chesson, *Las Vegas Review-Journal.*

had collected a small store of knowledge—we had become semiauthoritative.

The following paragraphs describe some of the basic aspects of the Gambel's behavior that were particularly interesting to us, and about which we felt reasonably confident of our generalizations.


Coveys


The social structure of the quail, if undisturbed by major outside influences (such as real estate development), appears to involve three separate levels or units: the family, the covey, and the supercovey. Each has its turn as the primary relationship, for about a third of the year.

The covey identification is the basic one and it operates year-round but assumes a subsidiary mode when one of the others is in force. Its continuous applicability is facilitated by a close association with a particular territory; generally the covey range does not exceed a thousand yards in any direction. From time to time, coveys fragment or disappear; new coveys probably originate with a particularly successful family.

The family units are established in the spring. Mated pairs move their chicks away from the nest as soon as hatching is completed and do not return. Each family unit operates independently, although they tend to follow similar routines in moving about within their common range. During the day they are considerably dispersed, drawing closer together at night to roost. After the spring season, individuals who were unsuccessful in mating, and couples who have lost their offspring or failed to produce any, recollect into a loose association, the nucleus for eventual reassembly of the covey.

By the time fall arrives, the conscientious and devoted parents have completed rearing their young, and the covey is reformed. Losses have been heavy, however, so that typically the group is composed of only fifteen to thirty adults. These now form a tightly knit community that moves everywhere together in close order. The coveyes are a familiar sight in many areas throughout the fall and early winter.

When the winter annuals begin to appear on exposed ground not normally traversed, the birds find the little sprouts so attractive that they are willing to venture outside their regular territory to feed on them. Often this is adjacent to the ranges of several coveys so that they meet on a common, unfamiliar ground, and soon they are moving together in a consolidated flock. Gorsuch felt that the formation of these winter flocks—supercoveys comprising a hundred or more birds—is nature's way of promoting advantageous crossbreeding. In any event, after they have enjoyed several months of communal feeding on tender shoots laden with vitamin E, the arrival of spring initiates a pairing off and a return to the normal covey ranges where nesting commences.

Mating and Nesting

We had little personal observation in this area, but there appears to be agreement on most aspects. As mating time arrives, a rooster begins following the particular hen of his choice, making displays or offering tidbits, and sometimes fighting fierce battles for her. Such confrontations may continue even after a pairing has been established. As far as we know, no study has been made to determine the probability that a previously mated pair will repeat, but one must assume that a certain residual preference carries through the winter months. On the other hand, losses are so high that the chances of both parents surviving any given year may not be great.

Once mated, the pair builds a nest on the ground, using whatever materials are available to form a shallow bowl in a concealed spot. Ten to fifteen eggs are laid, one each day or so. The hen incubates the eggs while the rooster stands guard at a suitable, distant vantage point, quite visibly on sentry duty. He avoids approaching the nest under any circumstances so as not to reveal its location. If intruders approach, he attempts to attract them to himself, often luring them away by feigning a broken wing. Twice a day, having made sure that there are no potential dangers about, the parents leave their posts simultaneously to rendezvous at an intermediate point. Then they move off together to eat and relax at a considerable distance from the nest. In a little while, exercising the same extreme caution, they return to their respective duties.

In three to four weeks the eggs begin to hatch; any that are still intact after a couple of hours are abandoned. It is important to get the new chicks away and eating—and learning to avoid danger. Scientists believe that late hatches result when one or more eggs do not physically contact the rest of the clutch; complete contiguity of the shells is thought to be necessary in order for the hen to synchronize the incubation process.

The late hatcher's chances for survival are generally very poor. On a protected and well-populated range, however, there is some possibility that he may happen upon another family before disaster can befall him. (We know of one who did!) In this event, he will be adopted without question. This readiness to accept orphans or strays has given rise to speculation that quail may sometimes hatch two broods—families are sometimes observed with two sets of chicks of different ages. The explanation, however, is certainly that one set has been adopted; authenticated cases of more than one clutch per year are virtually unknown, and the practicalities appear to preclude it.

There are so many predators and other factors that are inimical to the quail that one wonders how they manage to maintain their numbers at all. Part of the answer is a remarkable instinctive adaptability in areas of their greatest vulnerability. During nesting, for instance, if the hen is killed or seriously injured, the rooster will automatically abandon sentry duty and take over incubation, continuing in the mother's role for as long as necessary. Chesson observed one group composed of only two roosters with chicks—apparently widowers who had merged their families for mutual benefit in rearing the motherless young. Like that other "Odd Couple," they argued a lot but managed pretty well!

Raising the Brood

For about ten days, the tiny chicks are restricted to the ground, and the division of responsibility between the parents is particularly marked. The babies stay close to the hen who pays very little attention to anything but keeping them fed and warm. The rooster, on the other hand, is devoted entirely to providing a sharp watch. He is especially alert and suspicious, sounding frequent alarms. Although he maintains his distance, he sometimes appears to be leading or directing the general movement of the brood. Much of his time is spent up in a shrub or on a rock where he can detect anything untoward. Occasionally, when his family is well concealed or resting, he may take a few pecks at food but quickly returns to duty.

From the beginning, the parents, singly or in combination, are able to communicate a remarkably elaborate set of commands to their offspring. According to the perceived nature of the threat, the chicks are made to freeze in position, huddle under the hen, or scurry into the weeds. On more than one occasion we have seen them, while in the midst of normal activity, suddenly disappear. They will then remain in quiet concealment even as *both* parents fly noisily off in opposite directions to distract the intruder. When things have quieted down to a watchful waiting, the careful listener may detect their soft, barely audible peeping. In a short time the hen returns, and with her "all clear," the scurrying instantly resumes.

In only a little over a week, the tiny chicks are able to fly up to low branches, and the parents are quick to exploit this new protective dimension. Even in the trees, the chicks will become immobile upon command. Sometimes this may be for an extended period, however, and then one or another may occasionally change position to avail himself of a sunny spot (as long as he is required to rest anyway!). While they remain motionless, they blend into almost any background and are virtually invisible in full view.

## Food

Except for his esoteric tastes, Peep-Sight's feeding habits were consistent with those of the "real quail." Seeds, leaves, and insects are common fare, with the last constituting a minor proportion, especially in adults. The need of grit for the gizzard (which in poultry serves the function of teeth in grinding up food) varies from time to time, perhaps with current food preferences. Gorsuch was surprised to find that the Gambel's quail sometimes takes raw salt; Peep-Sight frequently enjoyed salted foods.

## Enemies

Beyond the harmful effects of civilization upon the quail population, it is clear that a great many are lost to natural predators. Losses are heaviest during nesting and the first week or two after hatch-out, when the quail are most vulnerable to small rodents, snakes, roadrunners, and housecats. Apparently, red ants will sometimes attack eggs in a nest or chicks that are hatching. On a year-round basis, the major enemy is thought to be the chicken hawk, but of course owls, foxes, and coyotes are also important.

## Calls

In addition to the sounds whose general significance we were able to fathom through our association with Peep-Sight, there are surely many variations of squawks and clucks that have special meaning. We saw considerable evidence of this as we watched the parents with their young.

On the other hand, as we listened to various roosters repeating the familiar calls, we gradually began to believe that each individual has his own recognizable vocal characteristics. Having Peep-Sight's call so clearly in mind as a standard, we would note the ways in which a stranger's call differed. If he continued for a while, we could determine that these differences were consistent for a given bird. Soon we became aware that identifiable variations occurred not only in pattern and phrasing, but also in timbre, pitch, tempo, accentuation, and regularity. Eventually we were persuaded of the existence of these distinctive vocal characteristics, and we even speculated on family resemblances!

## Domestication

In retrospect, we are more convinced than ever that Peep-Sight's successful adoption was a singularly fortuitous event, and that the odds against deliberately repeating it are tremendous. We strongly advise against the attempt. A baby quail is an incredibly fragile creature and one should not assume lightly the responsibility for his preservation.